W9-ACM-104

AL ON

AMERICA

AL ON AMERICA

★

REVEREND AL SHARPTON

WITH KAREN HUNTER

KENSINGTON PUBLISHING CORP.
http://www.kensingtonbooks.com

DAFINA BOOKS are published by

Kensington Publishing Corp.
850 Third Avenue
New York, NY 10022

Copyright © 2002 by Al Sharpton

All rights reserved. No part of this book may be reproduced in any form or by any means without the prior written consent of the Publisher, excepting brief quotes used in reviews.

All Kensington titles, imprints and distributed lines are available at special quantity discounts for bulk purchases for sales promotion, premiums, fund-raising, educational or institutional use.

Special book excerpts or customized printings can also be created to fit specific needs. For details, write or phone the office of the Kensington Special Sales Manager: Kensington Publishing Corp., 850 Third Avenue, New York, NY 10022, Attn. Special Sales Department. Phone: 1-800-221-2647.

Dafina Books and the Dafina logo Reg. U.S. Pat. & TM Off.

Library of Congress Card Catalogue Number: 2002101733
ISBN 0-7582-0350-0

First Printing: October 2002
10 9 8 7 6 5 4 3 2 1

Printed in the United States of America

CONTENTS

PART II. My People, My People

INTRODUCTION
Al on America

Today we live in a changed world—changed by the actions of a people who are willing to sacrifice their own lives to kill Americans and all that America stands for. We now live in a country on edge, afraid, battered, but still standing. Standing for our rights and standing for one another. This is a changed world.

For twenty years I have spent my life trying to unhinge policies that I felt were biased and unfair. I have marched for freedom; I have marched against injustice. I have been to jail and I was even stabbed for what I believe.

And on September 11, my agenda, my platform became an agenda, a platform for all America. When nineteen terrorists decided to turn our planes into missiles and attack the very fabric of our lives, America was forced to change; I was forced to change. It was no longer about black America or minority America. It's now about America.

The terrorists did not notify Latinos or blacks to leave the World Trade Center on the morning of September 11. They didn't call Asian Americans and tell them not to get on United Airlines Flight 93, which crashed into a field in Pennsylvania. They didn't send E-mails to Indian Americans warning them to stay out of the Pentagon that morning. Their goal was to kill Americans and send a message to America. Well, America got the message. We are the United States, like it or not.

People who hate America see us as more united than we may really be. On September 11, we had the unique ability to die together even when we didn't have the desire to really live together. But things have changed. We are starting to see people who couldn't walk together and embrace one another, now backing into one another out of fear. People are waving the flag in the hood *and* in the suburbs. We are showing more unity.

But that unity will not be more than a facade if we don't follow it up. Much like with faith, deeds must follow. For too long we have been giving lip service to unity and freedom. America is full of slogans. The most popular slogan following September 11 was "We Shall Overcome." I found that ironic, but I understood. Somewhere, somehow, America understood that if we were going to win this war on terror, if we were going to overcome, we had to capture the spirit of the Civil Rights fighters. They didn't go get Richard Nixon's song or Barry Goldwater's song, they got Dr. King's song *We Shall Overcome.*

I understood why America wrapped itself around those words. Those were the words that allowed a pregnant woman to defy the law and be sprayed by water hoses and be attacked by dogs while fighting against segregation. Those were the words that allowed men to be spat upon, beaten, and lynched and not fight back with fists but with spirit and conviction. Those were the words that allowed people to walk to work every day for a year rather than sit at the back of the bus. Within those words are actions that carried a movement. And it's time once again for each individual American to decide to do something as dramatic for the sake of this country.

On our currency and in our courthouses are the words "In God We Trust." It's easy to trust God. You see the sun come out every morning; you see the stars in the sky at night. If you get sick, you can call on Him. If you're down, He'll lift you up. It's not hard to trust God. The question is, can God trust you? Can He depend on you the way you depend on Him? That's the real challenge.

During the days following the terror attacks on this nation, the number-one song was "God Bless America." The question is, when is America going to bless God? When are we going to take care of the children, take care of the elderly, feed the hungry? God has already blessed America from sea to shining sea. When do we bless God?

A couple of weeks after the bombing I was doing a radio interview. The interviewer pointed out that at 8:48 A.M. there would be a national call to pause and honor those victims of September 11. There would be a moment of silence, and then radio stations across the country would play "America the Beautiful."

At 8:48, they stopped and "America the Beautiful"—the rendition sung by Ray Charles—was played. Ray Charles began to sing:

"Oh beautiful, for spacious skies
For amber waves of grain.
For purple mountain majesties
above the fruited plain.
America! America!"

And as I listened it occurred to me that Ray Charles wasn't singing about what he knew, because as a blind man he has never seen spacious skies or amber waves of grain. He has never seen purple mountain majesties or the fruited plain. But Ray Charles believed in a vision he could not see.

After the song, we went back to the broadcast, and one of the radio callers asked me about patriotism in the black community. He said, "After September eleventh, I drove through a black neighborhood and I didn't see many flags at all. How do you explain this, Reverend Sharpton?"

I said, "Well, if you drive through black neighborhoods throughout this country you will find that there are many things missing that you might find in white neighbor-hoods—not just flags. So don't take the lack of flags as being unpatriotic. Black people have been patriotic, fighting for this country, when this country would not fight for us."

One Saturday during Black History Month of 2002, two black brigadier generals came to the House of Justice during my weekly rally at our Harlem offices. Before the rally they presented me with a flag and they brought with them a Marine Corps band that played the National Anthem. The press who were there said it seemed unusual to have such a display at my headquarters.

What was unusual was that during their career these two brigadier generals went to foreign soils to fight for a nation that wouldn't fight for them. What's unusual is that they came back to a country where the people they fought against would have been able to eat in restaurants over here and sleep in hotels here that these black generals could not eat and sleep in—by law. That's unusual.

What's unusual is that the framers of the Constitution wrote that "All men are created equal," while they wrote legislation making slaves three-fifths a man and while many owned slaves themselves. That's unusual. It's unusual that Jim Crow was part of the law. It was not bad manners in the South for blacks to have to sit at the back of the bus or drink from a separate water fountain; it was the law. It was not a custom for blacks not to be served at Woolworth lunch counters; it was law. It was not simply a practice for a black man not to be able to fall in love and marry a white woman; it was against the law.

But despite these laws, black men and women throughout our great nation went to war on behalf of freedom for this country.

So when people question the patriotism of African Americans I have to take them back. I have to remind them that we, like Ray Charles, have been singing about a country and fighting for a country we could not see. Blacks fought in wars for the freedoms of people when they themselves lived in a segregated nation with limited rights, because they believed in the principles of this country; they believed that the America they were fighting for would one day be clear and visible. They had faith in this country when this country did not have faith in them.

Faith is being sure of what you hope for and certain of what you do not see. Many consider it faith because they believe things will get better. That's not faith; that's hopefulness. There's a difference between hope and faith. I had two people teach me something about hope and faith. Rev. Jesse Jackson said, "Keep hope alive," and that's good. But Rev. Adam Clayton Powell Jr. used to say, "Keep the faith, baby." That's what we must do. Faith has nothing to do with outcome. Faith has to do with what you know despite what you see.

I have faith in America.

But faith without deeds is foolish. I cannot sit back and just believe that America will heal, that America will strengthen. I must roll up my sleeves and do whatever I can, do my part to see that she does. That's how faith works. You can't sit back hoping things will change; you must be willing to step out of the box, take some risks, make some sacrifices for that change.

Individual terrorists were willing to make the ultimate sacrifice—with their lives—to spread their evil and make their point. What are we willing to sacrifice to secure our lives and secure our freedoms?

On May 23, 2001, I was sentenced to ninety days in prison. It was by far the longest period of time that I was incarcerated. And I wasn't prepared for it. I was arrested for trespassing in Vieques, where I went to protest our naval activities there. I went on the advice of leaders in the Puerto Rican community who explained the damage the bombings were doing to the land and people of Vieques. After hearing about it, I knew there was no way I could remain silent and do nothing. These same leaders stood with me during our protests following the brutalization of Abner Louima by New York City police officers. They were arrested right alongside me during our protests against the killing of Amadou Diallo. After hearing about the injustices in Vieques, I was compelled to stand with them. My move also strengthened a black/Latino coalition that went beyond politics and resonated on a street level. That had never been seen in this country before.

This was one of the first times I stretched my leadership beyond my base. This wasn't about African Americans. It wasn't even on the mainland. But it was still about justice and civil rights.

I went to Vieques expecting to be arrested, but I never imagined receiving a ninety-day sentence for protesting an injustice. Ninety days for civil disobedience seemed a bit unreasonable. But that's what they gave me. That jail experience ended up being the largest sacrifice I have ever made in terms of time. And it ended up changing my life. For a quarter of a year I was forced to reflect on what I was truly about.

I didn't have my entourage. No cell phones or two-way pagers. No people answering calls for me and giving me messages every other minute. No running around here and there. All I had to do was sit and reflect. This is where I decided that I had to change. I had to move beyond my own interests and the interests of my people. I had to work for the interests of all people and to recognize that all people *are* my people, too.

In that jail, locked away alone in a cell smaller than a bathroom, I had one of the most important meetings of my adult life. I had a meeting with Al Sharpton.

I had time to work on myself. I had to sit every evening behind those bars—secluded from the rest of the prison population, isolated from my friends, stripped of my family and loved ones and of every conceivable convenience. I went on a fast. For forty days I did not eat any solid food. I learned that if you can discipline yourself to give up an essential substance like food, it tests your will in other areas. It was a hardship but a rich experience that changed me into a more focused, more disciplined person—like a soldier going through boot camp. It was a test, a test to see how much I could take, a ninety-day crash course in life. And I passed.

I was a good student over those ninety days. I spent much of my time reading and studying those who came before me. I reread *Long Walk to Freedom,* the autobiography of Nelson Mandela, whose nearly thirty years in prison made my ninety days look like a trip to Disney World. He never wavered or cracked under pressure and torture. Nelson Mandela kept true to his vision. He kept his faith. And he was able to turn an entire country around. I read about Mahatma Gandhi, whose resolve to change a culture and fight for freedom and against injustices in India led him to vow to fast until death. Gandhi never wavered in his commitment to change.

I reread the autobiography of Dr. Martin Luther King Jr., who helped me define and identify the character of a true leader. Dr. King once said that there are two types of people: There are those who are thermometers. A thermometer records the temperature. And there are those who are thermostats; they change the temperature. A true leader is a thermostat because they change the temperature. They know what the climate is and they change it to what they feel it should be.

Dr. King was a thermostat. Nelson Mandela was a thermostat. Gandhi was a thermostat. These men were all great leaders. So was Winston Churchill. I read everything I could get my hands on about Churchill. I would consider his politics imperialistic. But he was a great leader. He was in a war and was able to step outside the box and inspire a nation to fight even though the odds seemed against them, even though bombs were blitzing them. Churchill was a thermostat. He even lost his prime ministership and came back. He changed the climate.

Fidel Castro is a great leader. He fought in the mountains by himself, sometimes with only three or four guys at his side, and took over an entire country. Castro is still head of Cuba, forty years later. He has been a leader over a span of time that the United States has seen nine presidents. Whether you agree with his policies or not, you cannot deny that Fidel Castro is a thermostat.

Ronald Reagan was also a great leader. I may not have agreed with him or his politics, but I don't think anyone can question that Ronald Reagan was a leader. He started in the 1960s with the conservative movement, stayed with it for twenty years, and went through being unpopular, being called an extremist, and stayed the course until he brought the entire country over to his way. Jerry Falwell of the Moral Majority did the same thing with his movement. And he, too, is a thermostat, as is Minister Louis Farrakhan. They are religious leaders.

I first met Minister Farrakhan following an incident at Temple No. 7 in Harlem involving two police officers who stormed the mosque. One was killed and it set off tensions in New York. Rev. Jesse Jackson called the New York chapter of Bread Basket and asked us to take a position. They sent me to represent them on the matter. I thought it was such an honor, a chance to show my mettle. But as I grew older, I figured out that it was such a controversial issue that no one wanted to be in the forefront. So I became the sacrificial lamb.

NBC had a black-issues show, *Positively Black*, that devoted a show to the mosque incident. I was a guest representing the ministers because no one else wanted to go on, and Minister Farrakhan was there representing the Nation of Islam. He came to the studio surrounded by the Fruit of Islam security. He sat down next to me and picked up the glass of water on the set and held the glass up to the light, checking it out. Minster Farrakhan said, "The Honorable Elijah Muhammad tells us to always check before we drink something." So I picked up my glass and checked my water. And for the next few years, whenever I was asked to be a guest somewhere and they gave me water, I would check it out, like I was doing something slick.

I've gotten to know Minister Farrakhan throughout the years; I even spoke at the Million Man March. And while I haven't always agreed with some of his positions, I will never disparage him as a leader. I think the thing that people don't understand is that he leads a religious organization, the Nation of Islam. And I think that in the context of that, Minister Farrakhan leads his flock well. You've got to deal with leaders in their context. He has never said that he wanted to do anything but continue the work of Elijah Muhammad. In that context, he has. So how do you grade him as a leader? It's like taking a math student and grading him in athletics. That's not what he's trying to do.

What's a leader? At the most elementary level, a leader is someone with a following. But just having followers doesn't make you a good or an effective leader. Effective leadership involves risk and sacrifice and vision. In order to lead, you must first have a clear picture of where you're going or where you're willing to take people. You have to be able to see the void in the system or in society and then try to fill it, and convince people to go there with you. The really effective leader will not just lead people toward a movement, but be willing to walk every step of the way with them to that goal. They will put themselves on the line with the people.

Dr. King did that. He didn't just call for marches; he marched. He got spat on and beaten. He was jailed right along with the people. And he had a following. During the bus boycott, he had to lead people to do something they had never thought of doing or wanted to do before—to walk or carpool for a year to boycott segregation. But people did it. And Dr. King didn't stop there. He took risks in areas that were not popular. When all other Civil Rights leaders were saying to leave the issue alone, Dr. King came out against the Vietnam War. That's real leadership.

A real leader never stops trying to bring people to where they need to be. I've met people who have established a following. But they didn't have a vision. They had nowhere to lead people. They were unwilling to take risks. Unwilling to make sacrifices.

A lot of politicians are empty leaders. They do just enough to get elected but have no real plan once they're in office. I know a lot of ministers who are just satisfied to have a big congregation. But they don't really try to change lives. They're hot for a season.

In this new millennium, in this new America, it's time for new leadership—leadership that focuses on building alliances and intelligence. We've spent too much time training and flexing our military muscle. That is obsolete in a terrorist world. There must be more alliances and intelligence and less tanks and bombs.

It's time for a leader who understands that our greatest strength is our differences. And being united—not just presenting a united front—is our greatest weapon. The next leader for this country must be able to look at all America and see her for what she will become and then work tirelessly to see her become it.

I am that leader.

PART I

★

AMERICA, THE BEAUTIFUL

CHAPTER ONE

★

MR. PRESIDENT

I was riding on a plane in first class to Phoenix in the early part of 2000 and I struck up a conversation with a man sitting next to me. Partway through our conversation, he leaned over and said, "You don't seem so extreme." He had heard so many things about me and I didn't quite live up to the billing.

"What's so extreme about a nonviolent Christian minister asking the courts and our judicial system to work for all people?" I asked him.

"You know, I never thought about it like that," he said.

There have been many misconceptions about Al Sharpton. I am not a rabble-rouser. I am not an ambulance chaser. I am not a troublemaker. I am not an anti-Semite or a racist. I am not unpatriotic.

3

I am an American who believes that America can and should work for all its citizens. I am a freedom fighter who believes that there can be justice for all. I am a father who believes that every child deserves the right to a good education. I am a husband who believes that women should have equal pay and that the government has no right to legislate what a woman can and cannot do with her own body. I am a minister who believes that morality and humanity are not old-fashioned myths but goals that can be realized. I am a person who loves people and believes that peace is possible.

And it is on those qualities that I am seeking the Presidency of the United States of America in 2004.

Now, the thought of that has made quite a few people lose their minds. "Al Sharpton, president?" "He can't win!" "He's not qualified to be president!"

Why not?

I spoke at Dartmouth University during Black History Month in 2002. It was so packed that they had to add seats. Now, I'm sure part of it was curiosity. But I believe that people want to hear something different. Many of the Democrats who are talking about running for office in 2004 are all reading from the same playbook. For voters it has been watered down to become a question of who reads the best. Who can smile the best at the camera and who has the best delivery and the straightest "presidential" posture. It has become about who has the most charisma. But the script is the same. The words all come from the same place. Presidential politics has become too narrow. It has become an exclusive club for white males, of a certain income, of a certain age.

When I say I'm running for president the response is, "How dare you aspire to do that!" But I ask, "How dare I not?"

To even question why I'm running is insulting. Pundits ask me why not run for Congress or local office, an office they say I might have a better chance of winning. That question, too, is insulting. If I'm good enough for Congress, why aren't I good enough for the highest office? It shows me that the question is more about assigning me to a place rather than whether or not I represent a segment of this nation and am worthy of leading. What they're really saying is, "Why don't you stay in your place?" Why didn't Jackie Robinson stay in the Negro League? Why doesn't Tiger Woods only play in Harlem?

Other people don't get the same questions that I do. No one asks, how can the Democratic Senator from North Carolina run for president? He didn't even finish his first term in Congress. Why does he think he can win? Because white males have no ceiling on their ambition in this country. No one ever questions their aspirations.

Who set the criteria for the highest office of the land? Article II of the Constitution states, "No person except a natural born citizen, or a citizen of the United States, at the time of the adoption of this Constitution, shall be eligible to the office of President; neither shall any person be eligible to that office who shall not have attained to the age of thirty-five years, and been fourteen years a resident within the United States."

Who changed the criteria? According to the Constitution, I'm eligible to be president of these United States. And I'm qualified, probably more qualified than any other person who is expected to be on the Democratic ticket for 2004, because I actually have a following and I speak for the people. I come to the campaign speaking a new political language—from a new playbook—that people want to hear.

A few months ago, as I was going through the airport in Denver, Colorado, I was stopped by a white woman who looked to be in her early fifties.

"I saw you last night on *The O'Reilly Factor*," she said, referring to the Fox News Channel show hosted by Bill O'Reilly. I thought, "Oh, no, here it comes." I was expecting a debate. But she surprised me. She said, "You know what, you need to speak for people like me. I have two kids in college and I'm scared to death. I don't make enough money to keep them going. There's no job for them and nobody cares about me.

"I don't agree with all of your politics, but I think you're one of the few people who at least cares about people and understands them. Do you think these guys out here running for president ever have to face a foreclosure on their house or ever got a delinquent notice from their kid's college? At least you know what that is. I want somebody at the top who has felt what I feel." And I understood what she was saying.

More than a matter of policy, this run for president is a matter of identity. The average person in politics today gets into a beltway mentality in Washington. They play more games with one another over minutiae and what's the insider scoop than they pay attention to what's going on in the cities and suburbs of this country. There are real people out there. We're talking about human lives. We're talking about farmers and office workers, contractors and store clerks, teachers and housewives. People are living in fear, and we have to break that cycle and offer them more than words.

I am running for president to finally put the issues concerning most Americans onto the front burner. I will force the other candidates to debate these issues—I mean really debate the issues.

When they talk about their welfare reform plans, they are talking about theory. When I talk about welfare reform, I'm talking about something I lived. When you hear Democrats and Republicans talk about welfare, they speak of it as if people on welfare want to be on it. Like people enjoy being on welfare and we have to work really hard to push them off.

I'm sure there are some people who abuse the system. But the overwhelming majority of people on welfare don't want to be on it in the first place, especially if they could get a decent-paying job to support their family. How do I know? I was on welfare.

When my father disgraced our family and had an affair

with my mother's oldest daughter, got her pregnant, moved in with her, and abandoned my family, my life changed. We went from a middle-class, two-parent household in Queens to a single-mother home in the projects of Brooklyn. My mother worked every day as a domestic, but what she made wasn't enough to support us. So we went on public assistance.

I know the humiliation of having to go down and stand on line to get the welfare cheese and the welfare peanut butter. I know what it is to have to stand on line to see the dentist—the welfare dentist. I remember one time the welfare office sent me to downtown Brooklyn to get a filling in one of my teeth. While in the dentist's chair, I was thinking that he was taking extra long with my tooth. When he was finally done he said, "I put a heart in your filling because Valentine's Day is coming up." Now for some that might have been cute, but for me it showed how little regard this man had for me. He never asked me if I wanted a heart in my filling. He didn't care about the extra time and if maybe I had somewhere else to be. He felt like he could do just anything because I was on welfare. And I couldn't do anything about it because I wasn't a paying customer. I had no rights. Yes, I know about welfare and what needs to happen to reform it. I know it from the inside.

The other candidates will debate their views on crime. I grew up in a neighborhood where we had to run from the cops *and* the criminals. I grew up in Brownsville, Brooklyn, with gangs like the Tomahawks and the Jollystompers. A lot of kids my age joined gangs because it was the family they didn't have at home and it gave them a sense of protection and pride. In these gangs they had an identity that they couldn't get from anywhere else. In their gangs, they could be somebody—even if it was somebody to be feared. They even made a living in their gangs doing criminal acts, from selling marijuana to snatching pocketbooks.

I was known in my neighborhood as the boy preacher, and despite the pull there was not much pressure from them for me to join. For the most part, they looked out for me. Many of them were my friends, and I would go to court with them when they got in trouble. I grew up knowing people in that climate, knowing criminals—many who could have been reformed and saved—who are now dead or still in jail.

I do not believe that the present matrix in America of detention centers is the answer. When I was growing up we had correctional facilities where they tried to correct behavior, turn people around, and reform them. We no longer try to turn people around; we just lock them up and throw away the key.

Prison has become such a huge industry for many cities and states that they are building bigger and bigger prisons, which means that they then must create a bigger and bigger prison population to support it. Before you even get to the jobs that prisons provide—from the guards to the maintenance workers to the groundskeepers—there are the multimillion-dollar building contracts. Most prisons are huge edifices, and whoever gets the contract to build them is set for life.

That's why the focus has shifted from rehabilitation to detention. You cannot tell me that politicians, who are responsible for creating the laws that lock folks up, aren't influenced by those multimillion-dollar companies who need the prisons to grow more and more wealthy. Those laws to lock people up make these companies richer.

We must eliminate that link. That's why in my campaign reform plan I talk about eliminating private funds. We must remove any possibility of corruption and injustice by not allowing big business to donate money to politicians. In my reform where elections are paid for by the public, big corporate donors would not have a role at all. None of the money for campaigns could come from the private sector or private donors. Campaigns would be publicly funded. This would take all of the questionable deals between politicians and big business out of the equation. And change the focus in the prisons from stockpiling humans to changing them into productive citizens.

I'm willing to debate these issues. And as we talk about reforming our prison system, we must also look at eliminating the death penalty nationally. Those running for president in 2004 will also debate the necessity of the death penalty as a deterrent to crime. But I wonder how many of them have actually watched a man being put to death. I have. And under no circumstances should our government be involved with putting its citizens to death. Not only is it not a deterrent, but there are far too many cases where innocent people have been put to death.

A 2000 study from Columbia University showed that two-thirds of all capital cases from 1973–1995 contained serious enough flaws to warrant a retrial. In retrial, 7 percent were overturned. And fewer than 20 percent of those retried who were found guilty received the death penalty the second time around. What if those cases had not been retried? Can you imagine people losing their lives because the cases had errors? Can you imagine people losing their lives who were not guilty? How do we give them back their lives?

Yes, there are heinous acts committed, and people should pay. But I believe that God is the only giver of life. Therefore, He should be the only one to take life. Clearly, it is a moral position I take that all lives are divinely chosen, so all lives should be dealt with in that manner. But that does not mean that my moral and religious perspectives would override the laws of the land. I would never instruct or allow an attorney general to break the law, but I will, as president, fight to change the law. Just as past presidents, including the current one, have fought for the death penalty, I will fight to have it outlawed.

And I'm willing to debate the matter. I am equipped to debate the death penalty because I've witnessed the government take a man's life.

In June of 2000, I was asked by Gary Graham, who renamed himself Shaka Sankofa, to be a witness to his execution in Texas. He asked for Bianca Jagger, local Muslim minister Robert Mohammed, Rev. Jesse Jackson, and me. Up until the last minute I tried to tell myself that they weren't going to kill this guy. I didn't want to see it.

I had never met Shaka Sankofa, but we had written each other back and forth and I knew his case well. He was convicted of killing a man, but he could not afford a proper defense. He obviously did not have the right counsel, and there was some evidence that he did not do the crime—at least enough evidence, in my opinion, to warrant another trial. Enough evidence to spare his life.

He had committed other crimes over the years, admittedly, but there was a question about this murder. On the morning of his execution I was scheduled to go to Detroit to meet with black auto dealership owners. I told my staff that I was going to Detroit and if they don't stop this execution, I will then fly to Houston. In my mind I was hoping that they would stop it. I've been to morgues on several occasions with parents who had to identify their kids, but I had never witnessed someone dying.

By noon the call came that they were going to execute Sankofa. I jumped on a plane, half wishing I had missed it, and flew down to Texas. Five hours later, I'm walking into the death chamber.

You can't prepare yourself for that. They bring you in—it was just the four of us and a Texas Ranger—and have you wait in this room. They told us that the case was going to the courts and that we would know within an hour whether or not Sankofa's execution would be overturned. The execution was scheduled for 7 P.M. Seven-thirty comes and we don't hear anything. Eight o'clock and we're still sitting there. By 8:30 P.M., I was thinking, "Great! They must have stopped it." But at 9 P.M. they come in and say, "The Supreme Court turned it down, let's go."

My heart started beating real fast. I could hardly catch my breath. They brought us down to the viewing room—a small, tight room with a big window. It was just the four of us and the marshals. Sankofa had his family with him earlier, but he did not want them to view his actual execution. Jackson, Jagger, Mohammed, and myself sat in this room in front of a wall that was all glass. On the other side was Shaka Sankofa, lying down on a gurney, handcuffed. He was kicking and talking loud.

"Make sure that we get my name as Shaka Sankofa," he said. "My name is not Gary Graham. Make sure that it is properly presented on my grave. Shaka Sankofa.

"I died fighting for what I believe in. I died fighting for what was just and what was right. I did not kill Bobby Lambert, and the truth is going to come out. It will be brought out."

Then it became real eerie for me because he started talking to us by name. "Bianca, make sure that the state does not get my body," he said. "Reverend Jesse Jackson, I know that this murder, this lynching will not be forgotten. Reverend Al Sharpton, I love you, my brother.

"All of you who are standing with me in solidarity. We will prevail. We will keep marching. Keep marching, Black people, Black power. Keep marching, Black people. Black power. Keep marching, Black people. Keep marching, Black people. They are killing me tonight. They are murdering me tonight."

While he's talking, they inject him with the lethal potion and his head jerks back, his eyes roll into his head, and minutes later, he's dead. I walked out after that in a daze. I could barely feel my knees.

It took me days to stop dreaming about that guy, maybe weeks. In my mind that could have been any kid I grew up with in Brownsville, whose only crime in that case is that he couldn't afford the proper defense. I felt so helpless.

After the execution I went back to my hotel room in Houston and I turned on the television and there was George Bush, who was governor of Texas at the time. He had a big smile on his face as he was addressing the press about the execution of Sankofa. And he stood before the cameras and said, "This was a great day for justice."

Justice? How do we celebrate killing people—particularly people who I feel were innocent of the crimes? How can we, in a humane society, act like it is all right to just take a human life? How is that ever a great day for justice?

All I kept hearing in my head was, "Reverend Sharpton, keep marching. Reverend Jackson, keep marching. Keep marching."

It's no coincidence that the wealthy don't get executed in this country. There have been wealthy individuals who have committed more horrendous crimes than Sankofa and we don't take their lives. The Menendez Brothers? Klaus von Bulow?

I'm running for president for people like Shaka Sankofa and others who have no rights or resources to save their lives and who have no one to speak for them. I am running to win, first. But I am also running to challenge the Democratic Party on these issues and more. I am challenging the party to come back home to its roots.

In the 1930s and '40s, the Democratic Party was an alternative for working-class people and minorities. It was the party of Franklin Delano Roosevelt and his New Deal. Before that, minorities—including my grandparents—were Republican. The Republicans were the party of Abraham Lincoln, and for many blacks it was the party of freedom.

What changed blacks from Lincoln's party? A. Phillip Randolph and those fighting for unions and fair wages came over to the Democratic Party because they represented a new deal, a chance for real equality. From Roosevelt's New Deal to John F. Kennedy's New Frontier to Lyndon Johnson's Great Society, the Democratic Party of the 1990s reversed fifty years of progress. They went in the opposite direction of that new deal. They began taking positions to the contrary of what Roosevelt, Kennedy, and Johnson were trying to accomplish.

The Democrats went back to pre-Roosevelt and became supportive of big business, deregulation of big business, anti-affirmative-action, pro-prison-industry, and other things not conducive to the protection of the working class, disadvantaged, and people who had no voice. My race would be the first challenge on a real, dramatic level to that shift.

In the 1980s the Reverend Jackson posed the biggest challenge to that shift in the Democratic Party. And through his Rainbow Coalition he was able to make some gains and establish a real liberal wing to the Democratic Party. After the 1984 elections, they established a counter to Jackson's Rainbow Coalition.

The Democratic Party answered with the Democratic Leadership Council (DLC). The DLC was led by folks like Bill Clinton, Al Gore, and Joe Lieberman and was set up as the anti-Rainbow Coalition. They said they felt that the Democratic Party needed to move to the center. They were successful in moving the party to the right mainly because of Bill Clinton.

As a Southern Democrat from a working-class background, he was able to relate to so many people—especially blacks. His style was more conducive to attracting the voter base they needed to win the White House. His style ingratiated him with blacks and the media. But in many ways his style betrayed black America because his substance and his policies really did not serve our needs. It's like going to high school with someone and even hanging out with them but really not sharing too much in common with them politically. That's Bill Clinton. He's a friend with opposing views.

A lot of people confuse Clinton's unique ability to socially relate with his policies. His policies led the party to the right, not to the center. And while I don't disagree with all of his policies, I believe there were many that were anti-people and pro-government and big business.

The onerous crime bill, which opened the door for the federal government to do the death penalty in an overt way, is one of those policies. Clinton's welfare reform policy was a failed effort to support the very people who supported him in droves—the poor. I believe the welfare reform bill attacked the poor and demonized them as people who did not want to work as opposed to being people who the government failed to train and provide with real jobs. I marched in 1996 at the Democratic Convention in Chicago over the welfare reform bill because I felt Clinton's policy was unfair.

People, especially many black people, got duped by Clinton. There are some who even refer to him jokingly as the first black president. Why? Because he could blow a horn and get along with blacks? I don't think Clinton's policies matched his social image.

Where Clinton and the DLC succeeded in moving the party right of center, they failed in delivering policies that moved people right of poverty. I am running to deliver policies that will give people not just hope of sharing America's wealth, but policies that will make the working class partners in that wealth. My movement is the next generation of the Rainbow Coalition. We are poised to take back the party from the people who took it from us.

I am running to take out the DLC, which I call the Democratic Leisure Class, because that's who it serves—the leisure class and the wealthy. They are pro-deregulation of business. They are openly anti-affirmative-action and pro-death-penalty. In many ways they are no different from the Republicans. I see them as elephants in donkey's clothes. You cannot fit a donkey's jacket on an elephant's behind, and that's what they have been trying to do.

The American people need to have a choice of directions. Is it pro-big-business or is it pro-people and dealing with workers' rights? Is it pro-affirmative-action or anti-affirmative-action? Pro-death-penalty or anti-death-penalty? Pro-tax-breaks for the wealthy or pro-one-tax for everybody? We have to have a debate on the direction of the country. Not a debate that says, "We're all going in the same direction; I want to get there in five years and my opponent wants to get there in ten years."

I'm saying that we're heading in the wrong direction altogether and we must change our course. I'm not debating timetables; I'm debating directions. I'm saying where we're headed is not where we need to go.

Again, there are those who will say, "Al Sharpton is not that man to take us there. He can't win."

In 1984, they used the same argument with Rev. Jackson.

And no, he did not win the election; he didn't even win the primary, but he made gains that would not have been possible had he not been in the race.

In 1984, it was Walter Mondale, Gary Hart, Alan Cranston, Ernest Hollings, Ruben Askew, and Rev. Jackson.

Mondale won the primary and lost soundly in the general elections. What did his supporters gain? Nothing. Gary Hart came in second behind Mondale. What did his supporters gain? Nothing. What did the people who backed Hollings, Cranston, and Askew get? Nothing.

Rev. Jackson forced South Africa and apartheid to the forefront of the Democratic debates. He made the issue of bias a national platform. He brought out issues concerning the military-industrial complex. He even debated the issues of drug quotas. He was instrumental in a nationwide voter registration drive that led to people of color getting elected to office throughout the nation. Doug Wilder was elected governor of Virginia. Harold Washington became the first black mayor of the City of Chicago. David Dinkins was the first black mayor of the City of New York—all a result of Jackson's run for president.

So did he really lose? Did those who supported him lose? No. We saw gains from Jackson running.

So it should not be a question of whether or not I can win, because only one candidate will win. But you had better have the right guy who can still deliver for you, win or lose. If you have the wrong loser, you can walk away with nothing.

At least with me, for progressives and liberals, I'm the only one in the race who, if you support me, will win you something.

But American politics have been reduced to racetrack betting. Voters have trivialized the process and hence have made their vote less powerful. We go into the booth and cast our vote for who we think will win, instead of the candidate that best fits our needs.

People don't go into the voting booth and look at the candidates and say, "I agree with this one," or "I share the same philosophy with that one," or "Al Sharpton stands for this and so do I, so I will vote for him," or "George Bush stands for this and I believe that also, so he gets my vote."

People say, "I'm going to vote for the one I think will win." Well, you ought to go to the horse races and stay out of electing public figures.

Your vote should represent what you believe in.

You should say, "I will vote for this guy because I believe in women's rights; I'm against the death penalty and I believe that prisons as industrial commerce is wrong; I believe in protecting Social Security and so does that candidate, so he or she will get my vote." That's what your vote should represent. It should represent you and what you stand for. That's why you vote. You don't vote based on who you think will win. You gamble based on those principles. Your vote should represent what you believe in.

I believe in liberalism. That's what I stand for. I am running to bring the liberal wing back to the Democratic Party.

Why not run as the Liberal Party candidate? Because currently the Liberal Party is suffering from an identity crisis. In New York City, the Liberal Party supported Rudy Giuliani in two mayoral races—against Dinkins and against Ruth Messinger. That's not a Liberal Party Al Sharpton can be a part of. It is a party of confusion.

We have to redefine what being a liberal or a conservative is. It has become whatever the latest commentator or columnist says it is. We have folks calling themselves liberal who wouldn't know liberalism if it bit them on the behind. We have folks running around calling themselves civil rights leaders who have never led any kind of civil rights cause and don't even have a following to lead. But if they say they're a civil rights leader or a liberal and the media backs them up, then that's what they are.

A liberal is one who believes in social and domestic policies geared toward people. A government run on liberal policies protects people, not big business. The priority is people-based. Rudy Giuliani was backed by the Liberal Party in New York City in both of his successful bids for mayor. But he did not embody any of its principles. There are those who will say that Giuliani brought back a quality of life to New York City. They will say that he was concerned with people and helped drive down crime to make their lives more comfortable. No, Rudy Giuliani used his policies to help make the city more business-friendly. Sure, he got rid of the homeless—they were bad for business. He cracked down on the squeegee men who would try and wash windshields at red lights throughout the city—they were bad for business. High crime is bad for business. His policies protected property, not people. And if people were in the way of making it better for business, they had to be removed. That's not liberalism. But it's okay for someone like Giuliani to be backed by the Liberal Party.

On the other hand, if you're a Democrat, you had better not say you're a liberal. Over the last twenty years *liberalism* has become a dirty word for a Democrat. It is slung at politicians like mud. This word *liberal* is not dirty at all. *Liberal* represents people who will be more than self-indulgent.

Conservatism as a concept is good, as long as you have something to conserve. But what does a hog farmer, who is in jeopardy of losing his farm because they have devalued what he sells, have to conserve? What does a single parent in Newark, New Jersey, trying to raise her kids on a welfare-to-work program that doesn't have a guaranteed job at the end of the program, have to conserve? What does a kid in South Central Los Angeles, whose education is lacking because his school district gets a third of what they are getting in the suburbs and who has a limited future as a result, have to conserve?

Some people can afford to be conservative. Most Americans, however, cannot because they have little or nothing to conserve. They need to be liberated—that's what a liberal wing must be about.

I've been asked, why not run as a Liberal? I am not registered to the Liberal Party. I am a registered Democrat.

Why shouldn't I run in the party that I am registered to? If I run in another party, I might create a climate to reelect the Republicans. Ralph Nader ran for the Green Party in 2000. He got three million votes. There are some who will argue that he cost the Democrats the White House. I don't blame Nader for running; I blame the Democratic Party. Obviously, there were three million people who Al Gore and Company did not represent. Those were three million people who the Democratic Party should have been speaking for and speaking to. If they had been, those people may not have felt it necessary to cast their vote for the Green Party candidate.

I believe that real change starts from within. I believe in working from within the Democratic Party for change. That way, even if I lose I have the option to negotiate points with the Democratic Party; then we can be on one accord, together, to defeat the Republicans with all voices being heard and responded to. I'm not running to destroy the Democratic Party. I'm running to build the Democratic Party, to strengthen it.

I'm running to bring liberalism back to the Democratic Party because liberalism works for the working class. Liberalism gave me the Neighborhood when I was growing up. Liberalism gave me Manpower Training and Development when I was growing up. Liberalism gave me afterschool programs. The kids today have none of these things and we wonder what's wrong with the kids today. The kids ought to be asking, what's wrong with us?

There is no program set up to take these kids' idle time and give them a sense of community and sense of employment. Neighborhood Youth Corps may not have been everything it ought to have been, but it taught us that we had to get up every day and be to work by 9 A.M. every morning. It taught us that we had a responsibility to polish our shoes and get dressed. None of that is there anymore.

The results are, we have a breakdown in family. And what are the answers? George Bush tells us our single mothers ought to get married. The answer isn't marriage. The answer is opportunity. I know plenty of people who have intact families in poverty. Bush's solution is like blaming the victim for being down. "If you live more ethically you would do better." Who lives more morally bankrupt and unethical than the very rich? The wealthiest Americans have a more wayward family life than anyone. But no one tells billionaires, who marry four and five times and leave children to be raised by nannies, to stop remarrying and having broken families. They're not painted and given the perception that they're irresponsible. To paint a poor person is not only insulting, but it is also a way of scapegoating people rather than dealing with the realities of the social order. I've gone all over this country over the last two years— from the snowcapped plains of Iowa to the cotton fields of Alabama to the sandy beaches of Miami, Florida, to the Hollywood glare of the West Coast, and everywhere I go, people are hurting.

I'm running for them. I represent them.

After the 2000 elections, a lot of voters were disenfranchised by the process. Many people lost faith in the system. Many were saying, "My vote doesn't count." My run will inspire hope and give those voters a reason to come out. I will bring out not only many who have never voted before, but also those who have just given up on the voting process. The Democratic Party will need people like me to restore that faith in the person who says, "Why come out? Look what they did in Florida," because that same person says to me, "I will come out because at least then my vote will stand for something."

CHAPTER TWO

★

WHY THEY HATE US

As I travel around the United States, I am faced with a difficult question: "Why do they hate us?" People want to know what kind of hatred would drive people to arm themselves, take over our planes, and drive them into the World Trade Center and the Pentagon—killing themselves. What kind of hatred would compel someone to call for a jihad against an entire nation?

And while there is no justification on this earth for what transpired on September 11—it was an abhorrent act beyond justification or explanation—the act itself must begin to open dialogue about America's history with the rest of the world and herself. What has America done to create an environment for such hatred, hatred that will drive people to be willing to kill themselves just to get at us?

27

In the Bible it says, "What you sow, so shall you reap." In Buddhism, it's called karma. The Koran and the Torah preach about some of the same principles. There is not a religion in the world that does not talk about retribution for acts committed. America is beginning to reap what it has sown.

For decades America, under the guise of "keeping peace," has gone into other countries and destabilized governments for its own greed and quest for power. We have made unholy alliances that are now biting us in the behind.

In the 1980s, Saddam Hussein was a friend of America. We gave him guns and military training to fight Iran. Now Saddam Hussein is our archenemy. In the 1980s, we were friends with Osama bin Laden. We provided him and the people of Afghanistan arms and training to fight Russia for ten years. Today Osama bin Laden is "the evil one." And Russia is our friend. I'm not saying that Saddam Hussein and Osama bin Laden aren't evil. I'm just saying that perhaps America made a deal with the devil that she cannot take back, and now the rest of us must pay for her indiscretions. America has turned friends into enemies at her whim. Manuel Noriega was once a friend. Then all of a sudden he became an evil drug lord who must be overthrown. We have turned people onto themselves, allowed for the killing of children. And now we are beginning to reap the same mad, inhumane, insensitive disregard for human life that we have allowed throughout the world.

The question government must answer is, why do we

make deals with people that we end up calling the "Axis of Evil"? And why did we help create evil that now is coming back to haunt us?

There is no justification for what happened on September 11. Those who perished were innocent victims. They were workers. They worked in Windows on the World. They worked for financial companies. They were firemen and police officers. In no way did anyone who died in the World Trade Center, in the Pentagon, or on those four planes that terrorists used as missiles deserve to die. And none of those people who perished were responsible for American policy abroad that opened the doors to September 11.

American policy makers had no problems going into parts of the world, whether it was the Far East or Africa or South America or Central America, and destabilizing governments. They would fund people who were terrorists fighting against the structured government. Now when it comes back to us, we cannot understand why people around the world see us as less than their friend.

If you grab my head and rub my face in the mud, when you lift my head up should I be happy? Should I have a smile on my face? At what point did we think that people across the world—people who have felt that America has been rubbing their face in the mud—would not look back and see us as the enemy?

In this War on Terror, the Bush Administration has identified the "Axis of Evil." These are the countries and nations who have supposedly harbored terrorists or sponsored terrorism against the United States. Bush is going around the world slapping nations with this "Axis of Evil" label.

We need to be very careful what we say and what we call people, because it is our hypocrisy that will be our downfall. We cannot out of one side of our mouth call one nation evil and then enter into a partnership with another nation that can be considered equally or even more evil—simply because it serves our needs. Bush goes to China, where human rights violations are blatant. Yet he calls North Korea the Axis of Evil. Pakistan is our friend today, but India is not. Why? On what basis do we brand a nation evil? By what standards do we rate them evil or part of this Axis of Evil? There are countries as bad or worse than the ones that the Bush Administration has placed on the list called the "Axis of Evil."

If we're talking about terrorism, there are many nations across the world guilty of terrorism that aren't on that list. If we're talking about human rights violations, there are many nations that engage in human rights violations that aren't on that list. Some of America's biggest trading partners are guilty but aren't part of the Axis of Evil. Who is deciding who is part of this Axis of Evil? George Bush—who openly embraces some of these countries that have a horrendous human rights policy? You can deal with the Saudis and their policies against women? You can deal with the Sudan and their slavery policy, you can deal with China and what happens over there in terms of human rights violations? How do you decide which evil joins your "Axis of Evil"? Are the other evil nations part of your non-Axis of Evil list?

Have the American people no kind of courage to ask the government these questions? Do we not have the courage to talk back? Today if you question anything being done by the Bush Administration, will you be accused of being anti-patriotic? They have reduced the American people to children and they're saying the boogeyman is coming and we have to just run scared. Right-wing politicians and the Bush Administration are saying, "If you're not with me, then you're with the boogeyman." What are we doing here? We're back to McCarthyism. We're saying, "If you don't agree with us then we paint you with the red brush." I'm saying we've come too far; we've progressed too much since Joe Mc-Carthy to allow them to do that to us again. And we've come too far as a nation to allow fear to create a situation of no return for us, to allow fear to make us hypocrites.

Why does the world hate us? Part of the reason is power, and whoever is in power is under constant threat of having that power taken away. If I were president, I would build up an intelligence unit that would allow us to really know what's going on out there in the world. The key to intelligence is allies. And to build allies you need to stop going around the world playing supercop and calling people names. You need to invest in other nations and build relationships. We don't go into Africa and deal with the AIDS and HIV problem. We give them a debt service they can never pay. We go in there and give arms and training to

31

rogues to overthrow democratic governments. We get on the wrong side of coups against democratic government. The reason why you have this anti-American flavor around the world is because many in other nations see America as anti-them. And they are so angry that they are willing to die to fight us.

How do you fight a man who is willing to die? You must make him understand that his willingness to die should not be used against something positive. But instead of reaching out, we come with a gun and threats. You cannot threaten a man who is willing to die. That means absolutely nothing to him. We have to understand what makes that man willing to die to get at us. There is obviously something there that we aren't getting. Instead we point a gun at the guy who is saying, "Shoot me; I want to die for the cause." And because we don't understand that, we go back and get an even bigger gun. That's just ridiculous. The bigger gun is not the issue. He's willing to die anyway. The issue is, why are we the cause? Why are we the object of this kind of decision?

In Israel there are now women and children who are strapping on bombs, killing themselves, and hoping to take out as many Israelis as they can. What's going on there? On September 11, nineteen men flew planes into our World Trade Center and Pentagon and knowingly (at least some of them) killed themselves in the process. What's going on there? You have people in the world willing to die for their cause, and our only response is bombs and bullets. That's not a solution—that's escalating the problem. I don't know everything, but I do know that there is more there than this government is telling us. I travel abroad a lot and I have the opportunity to see America from the vantage point of others, and I see that America is not without sin herself. And we do not have to go abroad to see that. As we continue in this war on terrorism and this fight to have homeland security, it's time for America to take a good, long, hard look in the mirror.

I think the greatest threat to America will come not from some other nation but from within. If you study history, you will find that every great empire from Egypt to Rome, from France to England, was toppled from within. They imploded. And if America does not begin to deal with her own internal conflict, she is in great jeopardy of following in the footsteps of the once-great empires of history.

Today you have unprecedented numbers of blacks in the military who couldn't get jobs, couldn't get training, couldn't go to college, who will be sent to foreign shores to fight for George Bush Jr.'s New World Order against the Axis of Evil. This is the height of contradiction. And it's part of the problem with America's foreign policies. America doesn't take care of its own, and it relies on the disenfranchised and underserved to fight for freedom abroad. I don't see any of George Bush's kids or nephews going off to war. I don't see Dick Cheney's kids or relatives going off to war. This war against terrorism is being fought by those who experience homeland terrorism. Before we send them off to fight for the rights of others, we must first guarantee that they have all of their rights here at home.

Those who will be fighting on the front lines are the same people who are left out of Bush's domestic agenda. Once again, blacks and Latinos are fighting for a country that is not fighting for them. Now, I'm not calling for black and Latino men and women not to go and fight for their country—that's against the law. But I do not think they should be volunteering to sign up for a program that has never had their best interests at heart.

The military budget has increased by 30 percent in 2002. Most of the expenses had nothing to do with terrorism but were things they were trying to push through for years. Bush has called for even more money to be pumped into the military, but the majority of that money will never see its way down to the soldiers; it will not dramatically increase their pay and benefits or protect them. Meanwhile, schools, Social Security, and other domestic needs are getting a budget cut.

We take money that we claim we don't have from domestic policies and put billions into building up the military. I think it is absolutely the most obvious contradiction to take a young black male from Detroit and put him on the front line in a country that is not 100 percent clearly responsible for what happened on September 11.

We are in a war, a war against terrorism.

But that war must be fought at home first. I'm not talking about Arabs and Muslims; I'm talking about America cleaning her own home first. For many in America, September 11 was the most horrific event in their lives. For others, terrorism has been a way of life.

Anytime a mother has to keep her children away from windows in South Central Los Angeles for fear of a stray bullet from a drive-by hitting one of them, that's terrorism. Anytime a black man has to fear coming home one evening and being shot at forty-one times by police because he was mistaken for a criminal and he "fits the description," that's terrorism. And anytime a person can work for a company for a number of years, trust in that company, and fear that their entire life savings and retirement fund can be stolen away by corrupt managers, that's terrorism.

September 11 certainly brought with it fear that must be addressed worldwide, but we cannot forget the terrorism in our own backyards. America does not just have an external problem with terrorists from other countries attacking her. America has an internal problem. There are two Americas. How blacks and whites view the same world is very different. America is two countries: one black and brown, one white.

You can see on Sunday morning, in our houses of worship, churches divided along racial lines. You see it in our public schools—more than thirty years after *Brown v. the Board of Education*, our schools are still largely segregated. You see it in our neighborhoods and where we live—there is an invisible demarcation line that separates the races. But more importantly, you see it in our perspectives and our outlooks. How a black person and a white person view exactly the same events and people can be as different as night and day.

Blacks and whites don't even watch the same television shows. In my Madison Avenue Initiative, where we fight for advertising for black media outlets, we have found that there are ads that can be bought on certain highly rated television programs that won't even be seen by the majority of black people.

There was all this hoopla a few years ago when Seinfeld went off the air. They made this big deal about the last episode. I never even watched one episode. I didn't even know that the show was on. I just didn't get it.

The way blacks and whites view me is vastly different. How I'm viewed depends on whom you talk to. To somebody white, I'm controversial, a troublemaker. To somebody black, I'm fighting for justice and freedom. How Rudy Giuliani was viewed by blacks and whites in New York City was telling. To most whites he was the savior of the city, who brought back civility and economic prosperity. To blacks, Giuliani was an unbending, nasty man who presided over a brutal police department that had to no regard for black life.

People in this country don't understand how damaging and how deep this division is. We are literally divided along racial lines, not economics—although that can be a great equalizer. But we are more divided by race. It may be a surprise to many whites that some of my biggest supporters are wealthy blacks.

One of the issues that I helped bring to the forefront is racial profiling. More middle-class and upper-class blacks are racially profiled than poor blacks. Poor blacks rarely leave their area. It's the middle-class and upper-class blacks who are pulled over on the New Jersey Turnpike and in Los Angeles. They are the ones driving the nice cars to their suburban homes in the so-called white neighborhoods.

They know racism. And they know it more bitterly because they are the ones who followed the rules, went to the right schools, followed the right path. They speak with the "right" tongue, even attend the right country clubs. But in the eyes of some they are still just a "nigger."

Until injustice and inequity is rectified in this country, America is standing on shaky ground. When we talk about National Security and Homeland Security, we must be talking about creating environments where every citizen can feed and clothe his or her family and have a safe, affordable home.

Justice and equality in this country will not happen until they are on the agenda of the leader of this country.

There are those who will question my run for office, saying that I only represent black people. Yes, that is my base. Any candidate who comes to a presidential run comes with a core base. Most candidates have a white, mostly upper-middle-class base and that's as far as it goes.

How can anybody expect to be president of the United

States when their core base is not as broad as the American people. My core base is not just blacks. Anytime I've run for office, I have gotten a significant Latino vote and even some white votes. And it's expanding.

I would say that my core base is more inclusive than that of anyone running for president—perhaps broader than that of anyone who has ever run for president. And I have a better track record fighting for all people than anyone thinking about running for president.

My base looks like the America that *is*. The base of the others looks more like the America that used to be.

FOREIGN
POLICY

★

CHAPTER THREE

THE MIDDLE EAST

In March of 2001, I had a debate on black/Jewish relations with a rabbi in a church on the Lower East Side of Manhattan. I told him that all of the tensions between me and members of the Jewish community were crazy. I had not incited Crown Heights. The incident at Freddy's was ridiculous. So we went back and forth and finally I got him to say, "Maybe you're right."

We talked about my work with the Jewish community after the Diallo shooting and about how so many Jews joined us in our protests at One Police Plaza—many of whom were among the first arrested there. We talked about how I was among the first to support the family of Gideon Bush, a young mentally disturbed Jewish man who was shot and killed by police in Brooklyn.

We continued our discussion and I said, "We have to find ways to seek common ground. We have to find a way to come to an understanding of one another." That understanding came for me on September 11. A young man who attends school with my younger daughter Ashley and who is also a member of our church, Canaan Baptist Church, came home with her that day. It was not unusual for him to spend time at our house, but when I came home, I found him saddened and overwhelmed with emotion.

His mother worked in Tower Two of the World Trade Center on the eighty-fourth floor. He had not heard from her since they shared breakfast and she went off to work that morning. Her body still has not been recovered from the rubble at Ground Zero. That's when terrorism hit home for me. Travis ended up staying with us for a month, and while he is now living with a distant aunt, he spends every weekend at our home. Kathy and I and the girls wanted to give him a strong sense of family and make sure he knew that he was not alone.

But his experience got me thinking about how people survive terrorism. And that's what led me to want to go to Israel. I wanted to talk with people who experience terrorism every day and live through it, trying to maintain a normal life. I wanted to hear their stories of triumph.

After September 11, I started thinking, "Now I understand what people go through in Israel and parts of the Middle East." They go through this every day. Maybe it's time for me to take a leap and identify with victims of terrorism—not deal with foreign policy, but deal with the concerns of everyday people, like the everyday people who are dealing with it now in America. The policemen's wives, the firefighters' children, the families of the waiters and waitresses who worked in Windows on the World in the Trade Towers, the loved ones of those who were killed on the airplanes and in the Pentagon. And people like Travis Boyd.

Travis had nothing to do with foreign policy; all he wanted and all he wants today is his mother. He didn't care if Bush is president or whether Giuliani's popularity ratings are down. All he wants is his mother.

So I called this rabbi and told him that I wanted to meet with some Israeli victims of terrorism because I want to know how they cope, how they deal. He said the only way to do that is to go to Israel, and he said it wasn't safe over there. He said the current climate might not be conducive to my going at that time. I said, "No, now is the time *to* go."

I think it would be a more important statement to go during a time of danger and meet with people. I mean, would there ever be a "safe" time to go? I knew it was dangerous for me to go to Israel, but it was more dangerous for me not to go. How can I preach unity, how can I be for justice and understanding and healing, if I'm not willing to make sacrifices—even the ultimate sacrifice—to see those things through? How can I be a leader if I'm not willing to go on the front lines and fight these battles?

Once I informed him that I would be going, we met with others Jewish leaders, including the World Jewish Congress and the Federation of Presidents of Jewish Organizations, to talk about the itinerary and to discuss some of the Israeli leaders that I would meet with while there.

I expected to be criticized by a lot of right-wingers for making this trip. But in these times, it calls for dramatic ways of reaching out to others in an attempt to understand and heal. And whether I met with all of the government officials, the fact that I was going to stand with the victims of terror began the process of putting a human face on victims of terror all over the world. We need to say to government, "As we continue our military actions, let's also try to reach out and have dialogue." I felt the best way to reach out myself was to go to Israel.

On the plane ride over, the former prime minister of Israel, Ehud Barak, was on board and we had an opportunity to talk. He said it would be important for me not only to learn about terrorism from the Israeli side, but he asked if I would meet with the Palestinians and appeal for peace.

When we arrived in Israel and met with Shimon Peres, he also suggested that we meet with Arafat. "You must meet with him and urge them to stop the violence and the terrorism." I told him that I heard Arafat would be out of town. But Peres said, "He's not expected to leave until tomorrow. Perhaps you can meet with him before he leaves."

We were able to get in contact with Arafat's people and schedule a meeting for noon that day. I left Peres's office and was escorted in a van by his people to the Gaza Strip. Driving through the Gaza Strip—before Israel bombed

Arafat's compound—it already looked like a war zone. For about two miles, from the Israeli checkpoint to Arafat's compound, we drove through utter squalor. The area was full of bombed-out buildings—shells of buildings. Then finally we arrived at an oceanfront—a beautiful oceanfront and a row of buildings. They were not luxurious but a far cry from the squalor less than a mile behind them. It was like a two-star resort on the water. This was Arafat's compound.

We stopped in front of his compound, and a contingent of security surrounded us. Now, we came into the region with armed security around our vehicle with sirens blaring, but these guys were clearly military. When we pulled up, there were press and camera crews everywhere. We were ushered in through a side entrance and came through a door that led to an open-air-type building. We walked up some stairs and through a doorway that had armed guards on either side, and into a conference room. There was a sliding door on one side of the room that led into Arafat's private meeting room. It was a big room that had two big chairs in the middle. It reminded me of a throne, but it wasn't raised. There were just these two big chairs off by themselves. Between the chairs was a table with a vase of flowers. I sat down.

After about ten minutes, the doors opened and Arafat walked in. Finally, we met and shook hands. Nobody was in the room but Arafat and me. I sat back down and he sat in the other chair, and there we sat in silence for about two minutes. I started wondering, "What's going on here?" Two more minutes passed and all of a sudden, the door that Arafat came through opened again and thirty camera people and other press rushed in, and I realized, "This is staged. This must be how he does this."

They come in, *boom, boom, boom, boom,* with the cameras, and then Arafat makes a very shrewd political move. He waits until everybody's got their cameras pointed on both of us and then he reaches his hand out to me. Now, we already shook hands and greeted one another, and I'm sitting there with a dilemma: "Am I going to shake hands or not? If I shake hands, I know it's going to be used by some. If I don't shake hands, it's still going to be used. They can say, "How are you here to promote peace and then snub this guy in his own place?"

So, of course, I had to shake his hand. He's the elected representative of his people. After they take their pictures, everybody's thrown out and we begin finally to talk. We talk about terrorism and what happened on September 11, and immediately Arafat denounces Osama bin Laden.

"Bin Laden does not represent Islam!" he said. He also said that bin Laden was one of his most vehement critics in the Islamic world. At world conferences, bin Laden used to attack him.

"Bin Laden said that part of these attacks was for the Palestinian cause," I said.

"He's never fought for the Palestinian cause," Arafat said. "He's just using us to promote his agenda."

About twenty minutes into the conversation, the sliding doors rolled back to reveal this huge spread with about eight courses of food. "C'mon, let's go eat," Arafat said.

So I'm sitting at the table across from Arafat, and Sanford Rubenstein, one of my attorneys as well as Abner Louima's attorney, who accompanied us on this trip, was sitting next to Arafat. For the first five minutes of the meal, Rubenstein and Arafat were talking about what garlic does to middle-aged men and how it keeps them healthy and virile. Nobody would believe that this Jewish lawyer from Brooklyn is sitting there talking with Arafat about the beneficial properties of garlic while I'm trying to deal with terrorism. And while this is going on, it's sizzling across the world that Sharpton is in cahoots with Arafat.

We continued to talk over the meal, and Arafat agreed to stand with me and declare that terrorism against civilians should stop. And he promised to continue to try to find those Palestinian terrorists who kill innocent Israelis and bring them to justice. Before I leave he tells me, "I have six or seven replicas of the Nativity scene made, hand-carved in Bethlehem, that I like to give to my guests. Will you accept one?"

"I would take it and give it to my wife," I said. "It will be one my gifts to her from the Middle East, because I don't have time to shop." Two days after we met, Arafat gave a similar gift to the Pope.

As I was leaving Arafat's compound, the press was still hovering. Arafat walked me out. He trembles a little because he has Parkinson's, so he walked holding my arm for balance. We held a conference and he made the statements against terrorism. The next day the headlines read: "SHARP-TON ARM IN ARM WITH ARAFAT!" Yes, arm in arm at the request of Shimon Peres, and arm in arm against terrorism.

Having said all that, the situation in the Middle East is changing constantly and becoming more volatile by the day. America must have a major role in stopping terrorism not just in America but in the Middle East. And in this region, given the amount of money that we give to Israel, we have tremendous leverage to say to both sides that the killing must stop. Right now there is a perceived imbalanced policy there.

The argument that Peres and others use is that Arafat either has something to do with the violence perpetrated by the rebel forces or he can stop it. That's what they said to me. And they said he shouldn't be a leader if he can do nothing to control the violence. That's a sound argument. You have to be able to enforce your side and have some power over the folks you say you lead.

But I think pressure must be put on both sides to stay at the table. I do believe that Arafat has to take charge. But I also believe that eliminating Arafat will not solve the problem, because there will be more extreme forces who have no desire to sit down and work things out.

When you go over there, the Palestinians and Israelis have the same concerns over peace: "How many times have we seen Jewish leaders sit down with us and promise peace? And you still have violence," the Palestinians say. And the Jews say the same thing about them.

I think somebody has to have a big stick in the middle and say, "Wait a minute!" We've done that, but now we have to be bold enough to make sure there are consequences for any violence that does erupt. We can pull out resources if they continue. We provide arms over there. It would give us a position that would be more solid if we said we will come to the table as participants in the area, and our continued participation will be based on what the results are there. We could help stabilize the whole area. Right now, no one is taking us seriously because we aren't using the leverage we have.

When Sharon was in the United States, he asked Bush not to recognize Arafat. Bush wisely declined. Arafat would certainly not want to be ostracized in the world and be considered Mr. Pariah. Colin Powell met with Arafat for the first time in April of 2002, and that was the appropriate thing to do. I don't think you can establish peace by talking to one side. And I think, in a situation as complex and as volatile as what is happening in the Middle East today, I repeat that the United States has to use its leverage to bring those forces together to talk peace. The whole war drumbeat of Israeli leader Ariel Sharon is not good for Israel, and it's certainly not good for the rest of the region or the rest of the world. It will not solve anything and will not bring peace.

Dr. Martin Luther King Jr. used to say, "If you live by the

eye-for-an-eye mentality, the whole world goes blind." If your whole strategy is to outkill the other side, then when does the killing stop? Especially when you're dealing with forces who do not care about dying?

Just as America was forced to deal with terrorists who were willing to kill themselves to kill us, in Israel that practice has become a war strategy of the Palestinians. It seems as if every other day a Palestinian is strapping on a bomb and going into Israeli territory hoping to take out as many Israelis as possible. And we're not just talking about men, but women and children are willing to give up their lives, are willing to be suicide bombers for their cause. It has become a badge of honor to die in such a way for a Palestinian.

And like America, Israel must find another way to get them to stop. Killing them is not the answer. Threatening them with death doesn't scare them. They're willing to die, ready to die for their cause; and in some cases feel it is their religious obligation, duty, and reward to die. So you have lost the ability to deter and frighten people by saying, "I will kill you if you don't stop" when they're saying, "I want to die."

You have to go to another step now. You have to find a common ground, a good reason why it is important for us to live together. America must come to the table with a position and program on what is appealing about living together for both Israel and Palestine. They are already at a point where they are willing to die together.

The first thing that must happen is the establishment of

a Palestinian state. The Palestinian state should mirror the agreed-upon land that was drawn out in the Peace Accord signed in October of 1998. Both sides agreed on the separation of land, and they should stick to that agreement. But now the hawks on both sides have agitated this situation beyond where there can be a rational discussion and agreement.

And that's why it's imperative that America step in with more than lip service. Given our country's investment in Israel and given the positioning that we have militarily in terms of the Palestinians, we can enforce going back to the original accords and go from there.

There are those who are calling for Arafat to step down, that his time has come, that he is ineffective and incapable of keeping an agreement. But how do you remove Arafat during this time of volatility? How do you have a transition under these circumstances to new leadership in Palestine? You have a man who is virtually a prisoner in his own compound, relegated to two rooms, and he was elected by his people to represent them. We can't preach democracy and here's a man who was elected. We can't just disregard his election.

And who would be the next Palestinian leader? The people who lost the election? When we got hit with the terrorist attacks on September 11, should we have said, "Let's throw out the election; George Bush can't lead us through this"? No. He won the election and he remains president. The fact that the Palestinians elected Arafat ought to count for something. If there's time for new leadership, then new leadership ought to win the election. But it's clear that Arafat must begin to behave more like a leader and work on terms that will not only preserve the lives of his people but create an environment for them to build a future.

The Likud Party, the party of Israeli Prime Minister Ariel Sharon, embarrassed him in May of 2002 and voted—against his wishes and the wishes of President George W. Bush—to reject the concept of a Palestinian state, not to recognize Palestine at all. This is an extreme and unpalatable position. And we must say so loudly.

Before going to Israel I met with several leaders, including Henry Kissinger, and all agreed that we should go back to recognizing the Mitchell Accord, which called for Israel to be protected within her borders and to pull out of more territory and make way for the formal creation of an independent Palestinian state with the United Nations peacekeeping forces to oversee the process. I think that any situation outside of this plan is simply a formula for more bloodshed and will only exacerbate war.

President Bush would be wise not to have the United States succumb to demagoguers—from either side—who have irrational views that they know will not lead to a resolution, but are only trying to play on the emotions of people for their own career development.

Bush must stop waffling on how to handle the Middle East. One day he is defending Sharon; the next day he is calling for a Palestinian state. Bush has the kind of leadership that, when he gets to a fork in the road, he chooses the fork as opposed to a clear direction. And that only makes things worse.

What the Middle East needs now are leaders committed to peace, who are strong enough to be consistent in their stance and not waver from what it will take to attain that goal.

There are people who have said to me, "Why are you involved in this? You don't know anything about foreign policy." And I have to remind them that I have been to the Middle East. I have seen with my own eyes what is going on there. I have met with common folk and national leaders. President George W. Bush has never been to the Middle East.

And when his presence was needed most during the eruption of violence in the spring of 2002, what did he do? He sent Colin Powell. Had the Bush Administration shown more direct involvement early during this latest conflict, we might have been able to avoid a lot more bloodshed. Even if we could not have quelled the bloodshed, a more solid presence would have set a better tone and given us more leverage and the moral authority to make a difference.

But Bush has not shown solid leadership regarding the Middle East conflict. Just the opposite. Bush ran on a platform as the faith-based president. During his run for president he touted his deep faith and moral convictions. He was the moral Christian anti-Clinton. Bush has been preaching and pontificating about his belief and faith and faith base, and sat back and did nothing while the Church of the Nativity—the birthplace of Jesus Christ—was under siege for thirty-eight days. And he never opened his mouth about the fighting there. George W. never raised moral indignation that blood was being shed, that war was breaking out in the birthplace of Jesus. And he is the faith-based president?!

We didn't even hear a word from the Moral Majority, not a peep from the right-wing Christians. When it came time to protect the birthplace of Christ, these men of God chose politics over their beliefs, which showed real hypocrisy.

If I were president I would have convened world leaders to say that certain places—like the birthplace of Jesus, the Western or Wailing Wall, and Mecca—are sacred. World leaders should come together and declare that certain places are off-limits to war and violence, that we will not tolerate it. If I were president I would have gone there myself—not sent one of my minions—and tried to negotiate a stalemate at the Church of the Nativity. But this president did neither, yet he poses as one who is so committed to Christianity. I guess Christ gets in his way sometimes.

It's going to be difficult to see a positive end come from this conflict in the Middle East. But I'm an optimist. As a minister, however, I know we're looking at The Book of Revelations come to real life. Anytime human life means so little that people will kill themselves to make a statement, that people care so little about human life that they will run planes into buildings and kill thousands of strangers and take themselves out, you're looking at the times that John wrote about. That's why those of us who have faith can speak at this time and know with certainty that in the end the righteous will be delivered. I have no fear at all, even in these times.

★

CHAPTER FOUR

VIEQUES

We flew into San Juan, Puerto Rico, prepared to go to protest the naval bombings on Vieques immediately. I thought I was going to go there, protest, and catch the next flight back to the States. But we didn't get in until about one in the morning. We were met at the airport after doing a press conference with some of leaders of the anti-Navy-bombers coalition. We checked into a hotel in San Juan, and the next morning they drove us out to this airstrip, where they had the smallest airplane I had ever seen in my life for us to fly to Vieques. The airplane was no larger than a conference table in a board room. Before that, I thought my trip to Sudan was the worst plane ride I had ever experienced, but when I got on the plane to Vieques I was scared to death.

There were six of us on the plane, and in between passing out, I could see the beautiful coastline of Vieques, which looked like a little virgin island from the sky. We landed and had to drive into Vieques and had breakfast at one of the cafés, which looked like a suburban Florida coffee shop.

People, just average citizens, were coming up to us, sharing their stories because they knew from the media that we would be coming. One lady told me through an interpreter that her children and the children in her neighborhood all had nervous conditions; they were very jumpy and traumatized because of the bombings. A lot of the kids had developed asthma, we were told.

After breakfast we drove out to the Navy base, which was about three miles away. Across the street from the base, protestors had set up shop in a couple of houses, and I went there and met with some of the leaders of the Vieques movement. Some of them showed me where they had been shot by wooden bullets for trespassing on the base. One guy had a bruise the size of a watermelon on his abdomen area. Another lady broke down in tears telling me how the after-effects of the bombings caused cancer in her husband. They shared their horror stories.

After meeting with the leaders, we held a press conference, where I shared some of the stories I had just heard. And then we prepared for our protest. We ran into a little trouble, though. The Navy, knowing that we were coming to Vieques to protest, locked off the area where most people go through the fence to get arrested for trespassing.

They were determined *not* to arrest us. So the organizers

of the protest put us in cars to drive to a place they knew of, for us to go through the fence onto the base. But it was tricky because not only did we have to outfox the United States marshals and Naval police, but also the media, who were trailing us wherever we went. We didn't want them tipping off the police before we were actually able to do our protest.

But the press was not cooperating. Whatever car we got into, they were right behind us. So I'm in a car and there are seven or eight cars behind us—all with camera crews. We kept driving and finally we parked in a place that was near a wooded area. The protestors got out and pulled down masks and started going through the woods. We had to walk about half a mile through rough terrain. I found out real quick what kind of shape I was in—terrible. And it started raining. So I had to do something that I never do—put a cap on my head. I'm running through the woods, and finally we get to where they had known it would lead to a fence on the Navy base. Somebody cut the fence and they pushed me to the front so that I went through first. I caught part of my pants on the fence and everybody was laughing, saying, "Don't let the photos show you with a hole in your pants."

When I got through, there was no one around. So I started walking toward a lighthouse several yards from the fence, and still no one. Finally this guy who looked like GI Joe runs down the trail with his gun drawn and says, "Cease! Get off the land!"

I looked at him and said, "Are you serious?" By now

many of the protestors—about sixteen of us—are through the fence, and here's this one guy with a gun. "Don't you think you ought to call for backup?" I said to him.

"Cease! Desist!" he shouted like a robot. And I started laughing at him and said, "You don't really expect us to take orders from one guy, do you?" So GI Joe left and ran back up to the lighthouse and I yelled to him, "Hey, you're leaving the criminals!"

In about two minutes a truck pulls up and two female military officers (both white) get out. One of them knew who I was and said, "Hi, Reverend Sharpton." And I said, "How are you doing?" The other officers said, "Cease talking!" "But she was talking to me," I said. "It would be impolite not to talk back."

"You're on government property!"

"Oh, that's true," I said. "I'm a taxpayer, so I'm on my own property."

By this time, cars start coming from everywhere, and about twenty marshals arrive with their guns drawn. One guy who wants to be a hero says, "Get on your knees and shut the f—up!" And he starts taking out the tear gas.

"You're going to spray us with tear gas?" I asked. "I dare you. Spray me first!"

"Oh, I would love to get you, Sharpton!" he shouts back.

But one of his partners grabs his arm and tells him about the cameras on the other side of the fence. He grits his teeth and squeezes the tear gas canister, wanting so badly to spray me, while his partner's holding him back.

Finally, they arrest us and throw us in the back of a truck that they used to transport chickens. It smells, and we're bumping around this truck the whole trip to the naval prison, which looks like it was built 150 years ago. It was made of stone.

They forced us off the truck and made us sit on the ground while they searched us. We're all on the ground near the barracks, and many of the guys on the base (who are black) start coming out of the barracks and run over to take pictures and get autographs. So I'm sitting on the ground, under arrest, signing autographs and hearing, "Oh, my mother in Maryland loves you!" and "My aunt in California is one of your biggest supporters!" and "My cousin in Chicago would love an autograph."

Then the commanding officer comes over and says, "Cease all personal photographs!" And when everyone leaves he says to me, "Can I have a shot with you, Reverend?"

"That's called military justice, right?" I said.

Then they fingerprinted us, booked us, and put us on this barge to go back to the mainland. We rode, lying down, for four hours back to the federal prison, and on that trip I began to think how serious this was. For us to be treated like this for civil disobedience, for the United States government to overreact like this—and they were wrong; I knew we were there for the right reasons. It was long overdue for the bombings to stop in Vieques.

The United States' handling of Vieques is one of the prime examples of our country's arrogance when dealing with regions outside of our mainland. It is the reckless disregard that we have for others that makes us a prime target of criticism and worse.

I got involved with Vieques when some prominent Latino politicians from New York asked me to get involved. They felt my involvement would bring more light and attention to what was going on in Vieques. For sixty years, America's Navy has been using the tiny island of Vieques as a training site—firing off bombs and missiles. For sixty years, the people who live on that island have been complaining, asking the military to leave, and no one would listen.

The United States, which calls Vieques the "crown jewel" of its Atlantic training sites, has said repeatedly that the site is vital to national security. That's a lie.

The United States claims its practices there have been harmless. How do you tell that to the family of that civilian security guard who lost his life when one of our bombs went off course? How do you tell that to a community whose cancer rate has mysteriously skyrocketed over the last sixty years? How do you tell that to the parents of children whose cases of asthma are also mysteriously on the rise? Harmless?!

But more importantly, it is wrong to occupy a person's land and refuse to leave when you are not wanted there. They don't want us there; we should leave.

You cannot say on one hand that we need to unite the world against terrorism and then on the other hand go into someone's backyard and pollute their water, blow up their beaches, and create an environment where cancer rates sky-rocket and asthma among young children soar.

It's a contradictory position. So when some people ask me if I changed my position on Vieques after September 11, I tell them, "No, my position has strengthened."

Sure, we need a strong military, but the exercises that we are performing on Vieques don't prepare the military any better for what happened on September 11. If anything, our presence on Vieques underscores the hatred that some have for America throughout the world, and we must address that. The type of preparation we were doing on Vieques does not and did not prepare us for this new type of war that we are fighting in the twenty-first century. What we need are allies and coalitions. We don't need to be making more enemies by using a person's backyard as target prac-tice. Obsolete military exercises don't deal with the new kind of threat we are confronted with today.

America should have left Vieques a long time ago—per-haps we should have never been there in the first place. My overall policy would be that America should never go where it will be detrimental to the people or to the environ-ment.

Bush announced while I was in jail in 2001 for my protest of bombings on Vieques that America would pull out of Vieques by 2003. His said, "The people don't want us and it hurts the people." So is he saying, "I know we're hurting you, but we're going to keep hurting you for two more years?!" It's ludicrous. If being on Vieques is wrong two years from now, it's wrong today. Why not leave now?

This is why we need activism. If Dennis Rivera, Robert Kennedy Jr., Adolpho Carrion, Jose Rivera, Roberto Ramirez, and I had not done what we did, it would not have been a national issue and Bush would not have been forced into a position to respond.

On one level, people are critical: "Y'all always out there making noise," they say. But that's the job of an activist. The job is to make the issue visible. If the issue is not visible, no one is going to interrupt their general flow of doing business to deal with the problems of regular people. You must force it onto the table. And that's what we did in Vieques.

CHAPTER FIVE

★

CUBA

In 2000, I had an opportunity to go to Cuba when a delegation of the National Action Network went to the Caribbean news conference. While in Jamaica, we decided to tag along to Cuba with some members of Congress who were going. This would justify the trip to Cuba because travel there without U.S. government permission is still against the law.

But Congress got called back in, so they canceled the Cuba trip. So we got in touch with the Cuban authorities and the Cuban religious affairs organization and told them we were coming anyway. They said they would welcome us, but they could not guarantee that we would be able to meet with President Fidel Castro. So the whole time, there was a debate going on in my camp over whether to go to Cuba or not. I finally said, "Let's just go."

So we got the whole delegation and flew into Havana from Kingston, Jamaica. We landed and were met by a delegation from the religious affairs organization, who walked us through customs. We checked into the Hotel Nacional, a very old, elegant Caribbean-style hotel—very regal. And it happened to be the same hotel Adam Clayton Powell Jr. stayed in when he traveled there. So I was really excited then.

They gave us a schedule of activities that we could do and told us again that the possibilities of meeting with Castro were slim. We happened to be there at the same time that they were hosting an international conference of leftist nations around the world (which we would call communists). The conference was held at the Karl Marx auditorium, which seated about 3,000–4,000 people. There were people there from fifty-two nations, and to our surprise, many of them knew who I was and publicly welcomed me. They had followed our fight against police brutality and applauded our work.

So we're meeting with different people and leaders and the whole time I'm badgering them—against everyone's recommendation—to see Castro. I knew I was supposed to be diplomatic, but we flew all the way to Cuba and I wasn't going to leave without seeing Castro.

I did my radio show on WLIB (in New York) and WHAT

(in Philadelphia) live from Havana, and I interviewed some Cuban officials as well as Rev. Lucius Walker, a black minister who had been working with Cuba for a long time. We talked about the embargo against Cuba, we talked about what life was like in Havana, and we talked about the educational system. And we also talked about one of my favorite topics—food. To my surprise, the best fried chicken I have ever ate in my life (outside of my mama's) was in Havana.

Cuba is very clean, and the only crime you could openly see is prostitution. You don't see a lot of dirt and crime. People even leave their doors unlocked there. It reminded me of the deep, deep South in the 1950s, where everyone greeted each other as they walked by. Even the cars were from the 1950s. Ironically, they were all American cars—Chevys and Cadillacs. It was like stepping into Mayberry with Andy griffith. I expected Aunt Bea and Opie to come running out any minute.

Even the nightspots had that kind of down-home feel. We stopped at one after we finished "Sharp Talk" and got something to eat. Mariachi musicians came over to our table and started playing, "I Believe I Can Fly," which was the theme song for my mayoral campaign. I felt very at home.

We stayed there until about midnight, and we were scheduled to leave the next afternoon around three. So, as we're walking back to our hotel, which is right across from the ocean, Rev. Walker pulls me aside and asks me what time we're leaving the next day. I told him.

"Can you have your bags ready by eleven A.M.?" he asked.

"Why?

"We want to take you all to the conference tomorrow, so bring all of your luggage," he said. "You're going to have lunch with President Castro. I just left him and he said he would like to have lunch with you before you leave. He said don't tell anybody."

"I can't tell anybody?!" I said.

"Please don't say a word."

So I go back and we get up the next morning and everyone is packed, but no one knows what's going on. We go back to the Karl Marx auditorium to the conference. They seat me on the front row next to Danny Ortega. We were the only two people introduced that morning. At about a quarter to twelve, the Cuban authorities came and told us to follow them. I told everyone in my delegation to come with me. They were all asking where we were going, but I couldn't tell them. So we get into a car and drive back to the facility we were at the day before. But this time it's different—there is military everywhere and the roads are blocked off. When my executive director, Marjorie Harris-Smikle, sees this, she leans over to me and says, "We're going to see Castro, aren't we?" I still said nothing.

They led my delegation out of the car and into the building. We get on the elevator that we got on before, but we go to a higher floor, which ends up being a conference room and a dining room. When the elevator doors open, standing there with no warning in well-pressed fatigues with his hand out is Fidel Castro. We shake hands and he says *"¡Bienvenido!"*—"Welcome!" in Spanish.

We ended up for the next three hours in a lively discussion. I have never met anyone with a more rapid mind. He was brilliant. He was absolutely awesome (and it takes a lot to impress me). He was probably one of the three most impressive people I have met in my life.

While we were talking, he kept looking at his watch and asking me what time my plane was scheduled to leave. I would say, "In about an hour." And he would say, "Good," and continue to talk, but only faster.

After we ate, Castro got up and said, "I'll take you to the airport myself."

We go downstairs and he's about to put us in his Mercedes, but his people tell him that our luggage is already in cars. He then orders his personal security to take us to the Havana airport, right onto the tarmac, and escort us onto the plane. We almost missed our plane talking to Castro, but he made sure we caught it. I sat in first class, and the pilot asked me to sit in the cockpit.

"I have been flying through here for eighteen years," the pilot said. "And this is the first time I have been given clearance to fly over Havana. They are going to let us fly over Havana in honor of you. President Castro wants you and your delegation to be able to see Cuba from the air."

And it was some view.

My trip to Cuba was enlightening and confusing. I cannot understand why a country with so much to offer us is still being shut out of the playing field. I found Castro to be a very reasonable, intelligent man. He is the leader of Cuba, and whether we agree with him or not, his little island can be very important to our continued growth and success.

There is no rationale that I've heard that makes sense to continue the embargo against Cuba. Many American developers have come to Cuba and have found tremendous economic opportunities that would benefit both America and the people of Cuba, and still there is no movement to lift the embargo. It's time. Our current policy against Cuba is outdated and deserves to be revisited by our government.

If the reason for continuing the embargo is because Cuba is still a Communist regime, then how does America explain its relationship with North Korea, and China?

When I was growing up, Russian leader Nikita Khrushchev was the devil incarnate, and anything to do with Communism was evil. The nation was on high alert for anything that even smelled of Communism. If it was thought that you sympathized with any communistic ideals, you were branded a traitor. The red-paint bucket was out, and people were being painted red left and right. Khrushchev was the devil and Fidel Castro was the devil's brother.

Today, Russia is our friend. Vladimir Putin is a good guy, a friend of President Bush and an ally of the United States. We have a relationship with Russia because it makes sense today for them not to be our enemy. But Fidel Castro is still the devil. How can that be?

When I was growing up, Russia was the absolute embodiment of all that was bad and evil. Now they are our partners, which shows me that the ideology and the political feelings and beliefs of people, particularly at that level, have very little to do with world and global business.

We talk about the human rights violations—of which I personally saw none. Yet we can dialogue with China and all of her blatant human right violations. We have continued to demonize Castro at the expense of good, sound foreign policy. It seems unwise to have such an adversarial relationship with a nation less than ninety miles from our borders. Why should we have a policy that differs dramatically from policies we have with countries that are far less strategically located in terms of meeting alliances—countries that don't share the same water space and that don't have as many people from their land currently in the United States? Why the hostile relationship with Cuba in the name of anti-Communism when that doesn't bar us from doing business with others? I clearly think it's wrong.

America's continued ostracism of Cuba comes into question even more under the Bush Administration. A lot of Cuban Americans who are anti-Castro live in Florida, the home state of the president's brother. There may be a political calculation that if this president changes that policy and lifts the embargo against Cuba, those anti-Castro forces, who are very powerful, will take it out on Governor Jeb

Bush. While I believed that Clinton and the Democrats in general were wrong for their Cuban policy, President Bush is allowing an opportunity to pass by for political and perhaps even personal reasons, and that's very wrong.

There is no small measure of belief in my mind that the alienation of Cuba also has an anti-Latino flavor. I think that helps the passions and emotions of some in the right wing to continue to preach anti-Cuban relations more than they would against others that are in the same ideological family in terms of Communism. I feel it's the same reason for our questionable foreign policy with Mexico, another country that borders ours.

Our whole set of immigration laws seems to be biased and archaic. They need to be reviewed and made more humane. I think we need to sit down and have a respectful relationship with Mexico where we deal with them as a partner.

Clearly, Mexicans are treated in a discriminatory manner by this country. We close the borders but allow a few to come here illegally, and turn our heads as long as they agree to be slaves or the closest thing to a slave that you can be. But don't let them come here with any self-respect or ambition. If they agree to wash the dishes in our restaurants or clean our homes or watch our children for the lowest wages imaginable, off the books, then welcome to America.

That isn't a foreign policy that will ever work for long. It's time to negotiate real deals with both Cuba and Mexico that benefit both us and them. Former President Jimmy

Carter went over to Cuba in May of 2002 to much fanfare. He went under the guise of fact-finding. He said he went in "search of an answer" to the question of how America and Cuba can resolve their forty-year-old dispute.

The answer is clear: America must end the embargo.

CHAPTER SIX

★

AFRICA

It is the second-largest continent on the earth and has the most natural resources of anyplace in the world. It is the home of oil, gold, diamonds, rubber. Its people have contributed so much to history, yet Africa is still very much an enigma.

What's troubling is how people from different lands have come and taken but not given back. They have stolen, raped, and pillaged and not replenished. They have carved up Africa and divided it so much that bordering nations can speak so many different European tongues. It suffers disproportionately from the AIDS virus, and not enough is being done to stop it. Civil wars are sprouting up in several lands, and yet no one is stepping in to find a solution.

We talk about a war on terror and we have a continent

living in terror. One of the greatest hypocrisies of the Bush Administration is that the current use of our military is for fighting terrorism. We only fight "terrorism" when it is convenient.

How do you have a dialogue with Sudan and not challenge them or use our might to stamp out their inhumane and diabolical practice of slavery? How do we talk about human rights in Cuba and human rights in Israel and Palestine but ignore the black slave trade that is going on right now—that I witnessed myself—in Sudan?

We cannot be a selective humanitarian. Either human rights is a yardstick used by the United States government—and it should be—or it is not. But it can't be used against Fidel Castro and not be used against the slave trade in Sudan.

America must strengthen its African policy—or at the very least create a policy to deal with Africa.

At the 2001 National Action Network's Keeper of The Dream Dinner 2001, one of the guest speakers, Coretta Scott King, called for America to forgive the debt in Africa. There is a strangling debt all over Africa imposed by this country, and when President Clinton visited Africa, he did everything but forgive the debt. We talk about aid to Africa in symbolic terms, but one of the most effective, dramatic ways of aiding Africa is to forgive the debt.

After we forgive the debt, then we must establish a real trade relationship. This nation's primary relationship with Africa throughout history has been one-sided. We've taken—

gold, coffee, diamonds, rubber, oil, and even free human labor—from Africa and haven't given much, at least not of equal value, in return. The second-largest continent in the world, the seat of civilization, has been exploited, oppressed, and colonized with the support of the American government and its interests. So we must forgive the debt against Africa because in reality our indebtedness to Africa—our moral debt—is much greater.

African Americans have been a pivotal, as well as inseparable, part of the whole American fabric. If we look at other nations based on their contributions to America, no continent contributed more to America than Africa.

America's first trade policy with Africa was taking non-paid workers, slaves, from Africa to help build the United States. The slave trade was a foreign policy. If you take that into account, it speaks for a new, humane policy toward Africa based on debt relief, based on investment, and based on a fair trade policy.

I've been to Africa several times. The last time was in 2001, to Sudan, where there were reports of human raids and a slave trade. I felt the only way to deal with this issue was to go and see for myself. I went to Sudan with a delegation supported by the National Action Network. We flew through Switzerland and hooked up with a Christian activist organization that had been purchasing slaves and setting them free. I witnessed the purchase of human beings, and I am convinced that there are slave traders selling people in Africa today. And I am equally convinced that slavery today is as onerous and vile and wrong as it was 300 years ago.

People argue that slavery in Africa today is different from slavery in America. But anytime people have to work for nothing, anytime people are exchanged like products and cattle, anytime you have a situation where women can be violated and have no rights, then you have slavery, and it must be eradicated and those responsible for enslaving those human beings must pay.

I also think that anyone who promotes or profits from slavery must also pay. In Africa today, Talisman Energy of Canada is exploiting the situation in Sudan. And while Africans in Sudan are the ones selling slaves, the Canadian government is certainly benefiting. And they are creating an environment for unrest and civil war that led to the slavery in the first place. Why? Money.

Africa, perhaps more than any other land, is overflowing with wealth. And if someone can get the current inhabitants into enough instability, they can secure the land for themselves. Canada would love to get its hands on Sudan because the land is rich with oil. There are billions of dollars in that land. That's what the value is there. That's why we have these really tumultuous types of situations in Africa today.

But for the love of money, people have put other human beings through unthinkable suffering and unimagined pain.

In 1994 I went to Senegal to the African, African-American Summit. On the second night of the conference, Rev. Jesse Jackson brought my wife and me to Gory Island, the primary place where slaves were held before being shepherded into slavery. Rev. Jackson had been there before. But it was my first experience and one I will never forget.

I stood in this tight stone passageway through which millions of Africans—my ancestors—walked. It was called the "door of no return," for once you went through that passageway you either died on the Atlantic Ocean or you ended up in bondage in America. And those who survived were my forefathers.

It is to that passageway that my mind always goes when the topic of reparations comes up. There are many who will argue that Africans are just as responsible for slavery as Europeans and Americans. And in some sense that may be true. But if you engage in a criminal act, all the guilty have to pay. If someone steals your television and I knowingly buy it, we know I'm going to jail—the thief and the buyer of stolen goods are both guilty. But with slavery, America took it one step further: she not only purchased stolen goods, she conspired in the thievery. It wasn't as if somebody had captured some slaves and sold them one time. It became a business, a policy.

So just as those in Africa have to deal with what their forefathers did to one another, America must also pay for her part in the crime.

The issue of reparations is not just based on the slave trade but also on the slave labor. America benefited from centuries of free labor. So the issue of reparations isn't about the trade, the process by which Africans were captured and sold into bondage, but it is about the fruits of their labor once here. It didn't end with the Middle Passages.

What a lot of people who are opposed to reparations won't deal with is the two hundred years of free labor that made America what it became economically. That happened after the trade. They are trying to stop it at the transaction, in essence saying, "I bought some slaves and that's the end of the story. I might be guilty of getting the slaves, but what about the guy who sold the slaves to me?"

They want to erase or ignore the two hundred years of working for nothing that made America the economic base and power it eventually became.

And the damage to those people who worked for free for two hundred years—the physical, emotional, and mental damage of enslaving people and treating them lower than cattle, are still being felt today. But if that weren't bad enough, America followed slavery with a hundred years of apartheid. The damage didn't stop with the Emancipation Proclamation. For a hundred years the descendants of those slaves could not go to certain schools, could not hold certain jobs, could not live in certain neighborhoods, could not even use public accommodations—by law. They could not vote, by law. And let's not talk about the things done outside the law by groups like the Ku Klux Klan to keep blacks "in their place." Let's not talk about the lynchings, the burnings and destruction of whole towns, the church bombings, and the terrorism exacted on those descendants of slaves.

When I talk about reparations, I'm talking about a debt owed people for crimes committed against their forefathers, crimes from which black America is still suffering. I'm talking about my grandmother or my great-grandmother. I'm talking about my mother, who in my lifetime could not vote until she was well into her forties.

So it is the height of insult to me for people to act as if, once chattel slavery stopped, everything became fair and equal in America.

We are talking about repairing the damage that is still reverberating from slavery and then the damage of legal apartheid since slavery that happened in our very lifetime. It is no coincidence that the education systems for blacks and for whites are still vastly unequal. And it's not because black children are inferior and cannot learn. The system is unequal.

It is no coincidence that the health treatment of blacks is vastly unequal to that of whites. A 2002 survey by the Institute of Medicine found that blacks in the United States tend to receive lower-quality health care than whites—both for serious conditions and routine services—even when income, age, and insurance status are the same. "Disparities in the health care delivered to racial and ethnic minorities are real and are associated with worse outcomes in many cases, which is unacceptable," said Dr. Alan Nelson, chairman of the committee that prepared the report.

A black family with equal education makes almost half that of a white family in income. The only way to equalize that is to repair the damage that was done. Deadria Farmer-Paellmann filed a lawsuit in March 2002 against Aetna Insurance, FleetBoston Financial, and railroad giant CSX on behalf of the 35 million American descendants of African slaves. One of the attorneys who is working on this case was the attorney who represented Holocaust victims. Many who received reparations were not the Holocaust victims but the children of Holocaust victims. And I support their victory.

Black Americans are the children of slaves. We are talking about the same type of racism here. There was no argument made when Holocaust families got money, and they should have gotten it. What is the difference here? Now, we can argue form of payment, but we certainly can't argue that the debt is owed.

I will not focus on the form of payment that should be given to descendants of slaves. Before we can even talk about money, first America has to admit that a crime was committed. If you stole something from me, before I negotiate whether I want it back we must first prove that you are the one who stole it. Then we can set conditions. The first thing we need to do is acknowledge that you robbed me.

Let's start there with reparations. Let's start with the fact that there is a debt owed. Then we negotiate how we can re-

pair it. What's fair? We can start with creating an even playing field. But we can't even get there until we recognize that
there is a problem. We cannot bring up the discussion of
how we will repair this, or what brings us up to par, because
America still will not recognize officially or even unoffi-
cially that the dead are owed. People are still acting as
though slavery and its impact was something in the past,
something that happened to my great-grandmother.

Let's look at it another way. If your grandmother stole a
million dollars and your family was able to build an empire
on that stolen money, do you owe a debt to the person you
stole it from? Or do you act as if you never stole anything
and you were able to build that empire because you're better than everyone else, because you're smarter and superior? And what if you raise your children to believe that you
are more successful—not because of the stolen money, because that never enters the equation—but because you're
superior? And if you create a system where those you stole
from will not be able to recoup that stolen money, but rather
must live as if—and be taught to think—that they are in-
deed inferior, does that not deserve some retribution?

But no one wants to acknowledge that such a system exists in this country. The detachment that a lot of people are
trying to have with the issue is fraudulent, and it's got to be
dealt with.

America must admit its sins in Africa and its sins against
people of African descent. It's the first step toward healing.

DOMESTIC
POLICIES

CHAPTER SEVEN

★

CHURCH AND STATE

J esus says in the book of Matthew, "Render unto Caesar what is Caesar's and to God what is God's." Even Jesus had a clear understanding of the separation of church and state.

I am a Christian minister. I've been a preacher since I was four years old. I believe in God and I believe that Jesus Christ died on the cross for my sins. My life's mission is to preach the word and work as an activist for the rights of the voiceless.

My personal views, however, will not keep me from being an effective national or world leader. I believe in our current system, and keeping church and state separate is certainly something I support and will live out. With that said, there are many things that I support that run counter to what my religion dictates.

I believe that gays and lesbians deserve to have the same rights as heterosexuals. I believe that sexual orientation should not be an impediment in the workplace, in the housing marketplace, or in the adoption market. Just as I would fight for a black or Latino not to be discriminated against, I would fight equally for the rights of gays. I believe that gays and lesbians should have the right to adopt. More importantly, I do not believe that the government has the right to ask if a person is gay before allowing them to give a safe, loving home to a child caught in the child welfare system. If you can't ask in the military, you should not ask when someone is trying to adopt. I know many gays who make far better parents than heterosexuals. Sexual orientation in no way matters when it comes to parenting—all children need is love.

My religion does not support homosexuality, but I do. I had a conversation with the late Cardinal John O'Connor a few years ago while meeting with him in his archdiocese office about various topics. He asked me why I was supporting and marching with the homosexuals who were protesting for the right to march in the St. Patrick's Day Parade. He said according to the church, homosexuality is a sin. I told him that God gave people free will. God gave people the right to choose—even to choose sin. That's why there is a heaven and a hell. So I will fight for people to have the right to go to hell if that's what they choose. I'm not here to judge. I was placed here to fight for justice for all people.

As a minister I am for school prayer, but I am not for imposing prayer on schoolchildren. I believe that just as children are not forced to pray, they should not be forced from praying, if that's what they want to do. I start my day with prayer; that's how I live. Why should the government tell me I cannot do something that is germane to my lifestyle? That's wrong. We need to revisit the issue of prayer and allow children to have the right to prayer if they want and not to pray if they don't. There should be a moment of silence to begin each school day, when children can either say a silent prayer, meditate, or do nothing. That's not unconstitutional in my opinion. But to ban prayer from school is not only immoral, it is as wrong as forcing school prayer.

My religion says that abortion is wrong. And while I may believe that life begins when the sperm meets the egg, and that only God should decide whether to take a life, I will not stand in the way of a woman's right to choose. If women do not have the right to choose, then it's a civil rights violation. So I would only appoint justices to the Supreme Court who are for women having the right to choose whether or not they will have an abortion. Now, I can believe something without having to impose my beliefs on others. That's true separation of church and state.

CHAPTER EIGHT

★

RACE

In his 1992 book, *Two Nations: Black and White, Separate, Hostile, Unequal,* Andrew Hacker aptly captures the emotion and reality of race in this country. In his book he asks a group of white students from various economic backgrounds if they could trade places under any circumstances with a black person—a superstar or wealthy black, even— would they? And they all said no.

Hacker established that no matter what was taken from those students, they would still prefer to be white, which shows how deep the whole notion of white supremacy and skin privilege runs in this country. It is understood, even if not verbalized, that certain people enjoy the benefits of skin privilege.

But we look around and see average white kids dressing

in hip-hop gear, speaking in hip-hop slang, and we all know they buy more rap and hip-hop music than blacks. And we see that as progress. But those same kids understand that if they pull up their pants, comb their hair, and wash their face, they can go back to being white and get the privileges that we black people will never get.

When I was growing up, Muhammad Ali used to say that everything white is good and everything black is bad. He used to talk about the hero riding in on a white horse. You have the president living in the White House. Even a kind lie is a little white lie. On the flip side you have the black market, black magic, and Black Monday.

And while a lot has changed in this country, while laws have changed in this country, that notion as a whole has not changed. Race and the issues surrounding race are still at the top of the list of things America must fix.

In 1986, a black teenager named Michael Griffith was chased in speeding traffic on the Belt Parkway in Queens, New York. His car had broken down and he and a friend walked through Howard Beach to look for help.

"What are y'all doing in this neighborhood," Griffith and his friend, Cedric Sandiford, were asked. And after heated words, a mob chased Griffith and Sandiford into the streets. In his attempt to get away, Griffith ran onto the Belt Parkway and was killed by oncoming traffic.

At the time of his death, I was leading the National Youth Movement, and our big cause was painting crack houses and exposing crack dens in the ghetto. A young man who worked with the Youth Movement, named Derrick Geter, whom we called Sunshine, called me about three in the morning following the killing. His cousin was Michael Griffith. In fact, Griffith had on Sunshine's jacket when he was killed.

"Reverend Al, they just killed my cousin out in Queens," Sunshine said. "Will you come over to the house?" I wrote down the address and went out there. At first, I thought it was a drug killing because we were out there fighting drug dealers. It wasn't until I got to the house and met Mrs. Griffith and Cedric Sandiford, who was chased and beaten along with Griffith, that I saw it was clearly a racial killing.

In 1986, in New York City, a young black man was killed for being in the wrong neighborhood. In 1950, Emmitt Till was murdered, lynched, for being on the wrong sidewalk in Mississippi.

We haven't come that far.

To many in America, racism is a thing of the past. It's something that happened "back then." To millions of blacks in this country, it is something we live every day. We know it exists—much to America's detriment. We must begin to have an honest and open discussion about race in America. More than terrorism, racism is a threat at the very fabric of this country, because it will kill her from within. Unfortunately, too many people refuse to acknowledge that racism even exists today.

We need a Twelve-step program to end racism. And as Alcoholics Anonymous states, the first step to recovery is first admitting that you have a problem.

No one believed in 1986 that racism existed in New York City. In fact, after Griffith was killed they said it was not racially motivated. But I knew better. I grew up in New York.

I knew the unspoken secret: that there were racists in New York who could make the Ku Klux Klan look like a social club. I knew the best way to show that Griffith's murder was racially motivated and not some "accident" was to go there. I thought, "Okay, fine. They didn't kill him because he was black? Well, let some blacks go out there and let's see what happens."

Sure enough, when we got out there, we were met with chants of, "Niggers, go home!" and all kinds of stuff. In fact, Benjamin Ward, the first black police commissioner for the city of New York, under Ed Koch, was there the Saturday I led the second march through Howard Beach. Benjamin Hooks, who was then head of the NAACP, was there with me. I had been very critical of Ben Ward because I felt he was out of touch with reality. But he was there with his NYPD to keep the peace.

We were marching in the street—five thousand of us— as hundreds of residents of Howard Beach lined the sidewalks, holding up signs and yelling all sorts of things at us. As the marchers got to one particular corner in Howard Beach, there was a chorus of young people, none of whom could be more than thirteen years old, yelling, "Niggers, go home! Niggers, go home!" Ben Ward was standing right at that corner with his battalion of police behind him. They had the barricades up and were making sure everything was orderly. But some of those kids were getting really loud and belligerent. Ward leaned over and said to them, "Okay, calm down; keep it down and back away from the barricade."

They looked up at him and said, "Who you talking to?! You ain't nothin' but a nigger, yourself!"

Ward looked shocked. But I wasn't surprised. I knew that would happen. And, of course, it only escalated when we marched on Bensonhurst.

But the outcome of my marches is one of the reasons why I will always be considered "controversial" in some circles—because I rip the veil off Northern established liberal racism. People can accept that racism exists in Birmingham, Alabama, but not in the North, home of the networks and Broadway lights. People aren't supposed to act like that in New York. My marches and protests exposed New York before the nation. Yes, racism exists—in New York. This is not just a Southern redneck problem. This is an American problem.

There will be some in the establishment who will never forgive me for exposing that truth. And I will never ever apologize for it. Because it was necessary.

The exposure heightened when we got to Bensonhurst. It was Howard Beach to the seventh power. We had more marches—more sustained, organized marches. The catcalls from the neighborhood were more vicious. And the reactions were more emotional than crazy. Bensonhurst was where I was stabbed.

Every day during our protests we had the same process: The police set up a special area behind a school to bring our buses in for the march, which was supposed to be our safe area. We would march and return back to our buses to go home. People from the neighborhood would be lined up on the sidewalks, some even in trees, and would be holding up watermelons and yelling and screaming, "Nigger, go home!" and worse.

During one march, a guy walked up and just spit right in the face of Moses Stewart, the father of Yusuf Hawkins, the young black man who was killed by a Bensonhurst mob because he was looking to buy a car in the wrong neighborhood. We were facing all kinds of hatred there.

It always makes me laugh when people say that I exacerbated tensions in Bensonhurst and Howard Beach. Like I went out in these neighborhoods and said, "Okay, now all you white people get together. We're coming out here at eleven o'clock tomorrow. Here are some watermelons. Make sure you throw these at us and repeat after me, 'Nigger! Go home!' " Like I trained them to behave that way. This is how these people felt. This is how these people were raised. This is how they grew up, and somebody needed to expose them. We needed to tear the scab off so we could deal with the wound. And that's what we did.

When America looked at that, they had to say, "You know, we haven't finished dealing with this race problem." Now, of course they don't like the messenger, but they got the message; and sometimes you have to take the flak in order to get the job done. I always use the analogy that I'm not the storm; I'm the weatherman. If I tell you the storm is coming, don't get mad at me; get your umbrella. But if you don't listen and get wet, don't say I didn't warn you.

Racism is still America's greatest problem. In many ways America's foreign policies—born out of racism—have generated a lot of the hostility we have faced. The result of that hostility is certainly deplorable, like what happened on September 11. But one of America's—particularly white America's—problems outside the United States and within is that she doesn't see anyone outside of herself. What they call a new world order is their misconception of who is actually in the world. Most of the world isn't even recognized by America—to America it's only Caucasian, European, when in reality the majority of the world is made up of people who are brown, black, and yellow.

America doesn't even see those within her who aren't white. And it is to her detriment. To ignore an entire segment of the population is like ignoring your legs. You won't get very far without your legs.

People have been lulled into a false sense that everything is okay in America. That we are united. We don't see the real problems. Racism in America is not about "Whites Only" signs and sitting in the back of the bus. It's more subtle and equally insidious today. It's found in its images; it's found in the language.

If you're shrewd and effective as a businessman and you're black and your name is Don King, then you're a crook and a con man. If you're a white man and you're Donald Trump, then you're brilliant and astute. Those are the racial linguistics of America.

If you're a young black man who built a solid base with no money, against all the odds, and you're Al Sharpton, then you're overly ambitious and a charlatan. If you're a young white man, you're a rising bright star. It's insane. The senator from North Carolina is talking about running for president in 2004. He never held public office before his Senate seat. He became a millionaire by representing victims in North Carolina. He's a credible candidate to run for president.

I've represented victims all my life (and have not become rich doing it), but still my motives to run for public office are questioned. We still have to deal with the subtlety of racism and how it's projected in America.

You have whites who have babies out of wedlock who never have to deal with the racial bias in the job market or the housing market. You have white folks on welfare (in fact, the majority of the people on welfare are white), and they don't have to deal with the stigma.

Redlining is a fact. That blacks are discriminated against when applying for loans is a fact. There is discrimination, for the most part, still in the job market. An average black family of four still makes less than an average white family. In 1999 the median income for whites was $44,366, while blacks earned just $27, 910.

Racism is the cause, according to statistics, for why health conditions in our community are a lot lower than the health conditions in white communities. Racism in the criminal justice system is the reason why blacks are disproportionately represented in our prisons.

When the issue of racism comes up in this country, white folks will tell blacks to get over it. Slavery is over. But it's not just slavery that whites must own up to. It was a hundred years of apartheid after slavery. My mother couldn't vote until she was well into her forties. We're not talking about my great-great-grandmother. I'm talking about my mother not being able to vote until she was grown in Alabama.

I'm the first generation in my family who could vote. I was born in 1954 and the Voting Rights Bill wasn't passed until 1969. What are they talking about, there are no more slaves? There are people in their forties who lived under segregation. And how did that limit them from social mobility? How did that handcuff them from opportunities?

Slavery isn't the only thing America had to repair. One hundred years of black people being treated less than a person is part of that whole paradigm, is something America must repair.

And until America deals with her race problem, she can never truly be the United States.

★

CHAPTER NINE

ECONOMIC
STIMULATION

O ver the past five years Harlem, New York, has seen an economic renaissance. Along 125th Street big business has moved in, providing high profile as well as jobs to the area. Disney, Starbucks, the Gap, a Magic Johnson multiplex theater, and even former President Bill Clinton now also have a Harlem address.

Many see this as economic empowerment for Harlem and its people. I see it just as another example of exploitation and hidden agendas. These businesses didn't move into Harlem as a favor to the neighborhood. They got tax incentives. And there is no lack of real business in Harlem. It is full of real consumers, who spend real money. It's good business for them to move into Harlem. These major corporations come in, they own businesses, they make money, they get a new marketplace, they take their money back out of the community, and we get some checkout-counter jobs. What's so empowering about that?

Real empowerment in economically distressed areas only comes with real opportunity. It is not economic empowerment to build a Pathmark in Harlem and then as your give-back hire Harlemites to work the cash register and stock the goods. Where's the empowerment there? It would be more empowering to provide the means for a Harlem businessperson to build a supermarket in Harlem. It would be empowering for these companies to have programs for job development within their companies, so people are not relegated to entry-level and low-paying jobs. There's absolutely nothing wrong with working the checkout counter or being a stock person or a concession-stand worker in a movie theater, but it's clearly not a position of empowerment.

In terms of Harlem and other urban neighborhoods throughout the country, a balance must be struck, one that will raise the indigenous community people toward business ownership and entrepreneurship instead of simply a job. We should be investing empowerment-zone money in those people who live in these neighborhoods. We should be investing in creating entrepreneurs out of them, not just bringing Bugs Bunny to Harlem and acting like that's progress.

When you hear people like me protest Disney and the like coming to Harlem, the issue isn't whether or not Disney should be in Harlem, because Disney should; the issue is, what are we doing to empower the people of Harlem, because Disney does not? If you are going to use the tax base of Harlem to invest in entrepreneurship, why not invest in Harlemites? Why use the tax base to invest in national chains who are already wealthy and who are only using Harlem to get another marketplace to sell their wares.

If I went to Howard Beach, a predominantly white ethnic neighborhood in Queens, and said I am setting up an empowerment zone, and I give Sylvia's a bunch of money to open a soul food restaurant there and give a loan to a black-owned oil company to open a business there and I totally ignore the residents of Howard Beach, they would take bats and run me out of town. Why should Harlemites not have the same pride and ask, "What are you going to do for us?" It has nothing to do with race and everything to do with respect.

When government talks about economic stimulus and economic empowerment, they must invest in creation of businesses and creation of jobs and job training for people living in those depressed neighborhoods.

One area that could be particularly successful in creating better opportunities for people is in neighborhood infrastructures. The fact of the matter is that you have severe problems with infrastructure all over the country. There is a need to repair highways, roadways, bridges, and tunnels. If young people are being trained to do this sort of work and we pay them while we train them, we would create a whole new segment of gainfully employed people who can then empower themselves. Not only would we be providing thousands of jobs, but we would also be doing something that is needed. And it would not be a handout or some sort of government welfare program, because these repairs are a necessity. Someone eventually has to do it.

The government has to come up with work programs to put work that is needed together with people who need work. We have become far too dependent on the "trickle-down" theory—putting money at the top in the hands of the already wealthy, hoping they will spread it around, instead of giving it where it's needed. Where you create the job, you don't need to trickle it down. Put it right there. Training programs, and doing something that's needed in the country like repairing the infrastructure, cuts out the middle man.

The problem has been government's wrongheaded psychology when dealing with big business. They think if we support business and strengthen them, then it will trickle down to the people. That theory didn't work with Reaganomics and it ain't working now. Wealth rarely trickles down to the people. Corporations use that political matrix to enhance their greed rather than address people's needs. Big business has proven that it has to be forced, usually through legislation and litigation, to give up any of its money. Even then, it's still a fight.

Citibank, which is now Citigroup, has been, in my opinion, notorious for predatory lending and redlining, discriminating against blacks and Latinos on home and business loan applications. According to the 1999 Metropolitan Statistical Area (MSA), Citicorp Mortgage made 385 conventional home loans to whites compared to only 86 to blacks in Washington, D.C. In D.C. blacks were 3.11 times more frequently denied home loans than whites.

In the New York City MSA in 1999, 1,236 whites qualified for a conventional home loan from Citicorp Mortgage while only 58 Latinos and 56 blacks qualified. Blacks were denied loans 3.31 times more frequently than whites by Citicorp in New York. Nationwide, Citigroup denied African Americans three times more frequently than whites, versus the industry's two-to-one standard.

In addition to denying minorities loans, I believe Citigroup was responsible for saddling blacks and Latinos with high-interest loans—at a much higher rate than they offered to whites. Citigroup, now Citifinancial after the merger with Travelers, offers minorities an "opportunity" to own their own home or business, but they make it so prohibitive with high interest rates, high points, prepayment penalties, and other costs not imposed on their conventional loans, that people rarely, if ever, really own their home or business. They become, in essence, permanent renters. I know many people who end up losing their homes altogether because they cannot keep up with the ever-increasing payments.

Dealing with banks like Citigroup is like dealing with a loan shark. And there's no program in place for people who clean up their credit to go back and renegotiate the loans. It's not right and it's not empowering.

Government's role is to protect citizens and not be an aid to major industry under the guise that major industry will ultimately do what's good for the citizens when they are set up for private profit, *not* public service. Government should be by the people, for the people. But for too long government has been about special interest groups and corporate welfare. Government serves the rich and has become an agent of the wealthy.

A prime example of this was Enron.

The Enron situation is clearly indicative of how the wealthy can manipulate the system at the expense of working-class people. Enron's contributions to the Democrats and the Republicans were not some act of civic duty. They wanted to have an influence on deregulation. By deregulating the energy industry, Enron was able to set up these schemes that led to the biggest bankruptcy case, and potentially the largest case of corporate corruption, in the history of this country.

The president and the corporate elite are preaching and propagating this trickle-down theory today as they did during the Reagan era. It does not benefit or address America and all its needs. The trickle-down mindset leads to the creation of business debacles like Enron and Global Crossings and the abuse of common workers.

The government gives corporations money to bail them

out of financial troubles. They bailed out Chrysler; they have bailed out the airlines. They came with emergency grants to keep them afloat. More recently, Bush had a proposal to give certain corporations a fifteen-year refund on taxes as a so-called economic stimulus.

The government cannot only have resources to help corporate America. If government aid to poor people is wrong, then government aide to rich people is doubly wrong. Because the notion that those rich companies will make sure that the wealth makes it to the poor has simply not worked. In fact, the rich get greedy and the rich get richer.

Enron could not have happened without the aiding and abetting of government regulators and the use of all kinds of loopholes in the law that were not closed because lawmakers had a motive to look the other way.

What they did was tantamount to the shell game or three-card monty. As a political leader you cannot allow a company to declare assets under one company and liabilities under another. I know that game well. I grew up in New York City, where three-card monty was a very popular version of the shell game. You had three cards and you had to guess where the red card was. Enron played a corporate game of three-card monty, and we had to guess which company had the liabilities. It was crazy.

When I was running for the Senate, I had to disclose all of my finances and taxes. It was a surprise to most people because they assumed I had all of this money and was hiding it, and it would surely come out with my tax disclosure. It did not. First of all, my value system does not require that I become a multimillionaire. I'm not opposed to people accumulating wealth. But I've never accumulated wealth, because most of what I have earned from my speaking and writing I've used to educate my kids and sustain a home base. There are always tabloid stories asking if I'm wealthy. First of all, there would be nothing wrong if I were wealthy, but I'm not.

I have run for office several times, and every time people were saying, "Oh, wait until he gives his financial disclosure. Just wait." But each time they were disappointed. I have no real assets. There are no hidden homes in the Bahamas with another in Europe. What you see is what you get. The fact of the matter is, for the first few years of the National Action Network I had to lend the Network money. I would go out and preach on a Sunday or do lunch at a college, which was my personal fee, and lend money to the Network to make payroll. But I believe that if you don't believe in what you are doing, then why should anybody else believe in it? Why would somebody else donate or lend the organization money if I'm not willing to? So I think it's a matter of deciding early what you consider wealth—your work or owning some buildings. Do you want to get rich? Is that your main objective, at any cost? Too many businesses choose the latter.

I've even been accused of not paying enough taxes. I

know I have paid more taxes than Enron, and Enron's employees probably paid more taxes than Enron, too.

Enron was able to use loopholes under the guise that it's good for the economy. It's not good for the economy—only their private wealth. And as president I will make sure there is a tax structure that is fair for everyone. I will not have tax structures set up that would in effect subsidize and be welfare to corporations.

I went to Houston to meet with the former Enron workers. I was on my way to Raleigh, North Carolina, to visit a chapter of the National Action Network (NAN), when I got the call from Rev. James Dixon, president of the Texas branch of NAN.

Reverend Dixon had earlier brought me into Jasper, Texas, to speak at the funeral of James Byrd, the man who was dragged by three white men behind a pickup truck until his torso was ripped from the rest of his body. Rev. Dixon told me that they needed me in Texas for Enron.

"Well, of course everybody's heard of the scandal," I said. "But why should I come?"

At the time I didn't know all of the details, and I wasn't aware of just how many people were affected by this scandal. Rev. Dixon told me that many of the members of his church were Enron employees.

I decided to go to Houston. I knew people would look at that and say, "Oh, there goes Sharpton in Texas, jumping into a hot issue." But it was the members of Faith Baptist

Church, the members of Rev. Joe Ratliff's church and those of Rev. Kirby John's—people I had worked with over the years—who were calling for me to come.

I didn't go there to support my buddies who ran Enron, because I didn't know anyone who ran Enron. I went there for the hardworking people whose lives were thrown into the balance by corruption and irresponsibility. I went for people who didn't have anyone to speak for them. They needed a voice.

If the government can look at bailing out Chrysler or American Airlines, why couldn't the government come up with immediate relief for these people?

I met with some of the victims at the Rib House. One lady, a single mother, said she had been saving since she began working at Enron toward a college fund for her son. And, of course, she was saving for her retirement. She had amassed more than $300,000 in her 401K. Now she has nothing.

While in Houston, we called for public hearings and lawsuits. We got some of the best legal minds we could find—Johnnie Cochran and Lou Meyers—to represent these people. The Ken Lays of the world would never have a problem finding good legal representation. They have all the money in the world.

But who was going to stand up for Jane Smith, who now can't pay her mortgage or her child's tuition? And she invested her money to do so. She wasn't irresponsible. She wasn't out partying and finger-poppin'. She invested her money in her 401K at her job that the government said was a stable business. Now she's left holding the bag. And people are giving comfort to Pharaoh while fighting the Israelites.

As president, I will focus on building the economy through building up people.

Consumer Provisions/ Economic Stimulation:

1. Homeowner incentives, such as microloans in empowerment zones, lower interest rates, tax deductions for renters directed into escrow accounts to be applied to the purchases of homes

2. Federally guaranteed home value insurance for homes purchased in empowerment zones to ensure against drops in values and encourage development in unstable neighborhoods

3. Credit card industry regulation (preventing this industry from predatory tactics toward low-income families, preventing usurious interest rates). Have the government "nationalize" these industries by providing government-issued fair loans and fair credit card offerings to low-income families

4. Massive consumer-favorable antitrust enforcement (starting with media and communication companies, banks, etc.)

Increasing Revenue for the Federal Government:

1. Terminate subsidies to the sugar industry

2. Terminate tax breaks and subsidies to the tobacco industry

3. Terminate tax avoidance opportunities in offshore bank accounts and corporations

4. Eliminate estate taxes for estates under $500,000 while *increasing* estate taxes for estates over $1,000,000 (Note the fiction for PR purposes: there are already no taxes for estates under $675,000, but the public is generally not aware of this.)

5. Demand rent for slices of the broadcast spectrum from the industries using them (those that the government should have charged money for originally)

6. Adjust military spending to focus on intelligently winning the war on terrorism; reduce spending on expensive programs of questionable value, such as star wars, that primarily feed the military-industrial complex

7. Reduce excessive government expenditures on the prison-industrial complex by revising minimum sentencing provisions and refocusing antidrug policy from incarceration to treatment

CHAPTER TEN

★

NATIONAL HEALTH CARE AND AIDS

In 1999, the Patients' Bill of Rights was introduced by Senate Democratic Leader Tom Daschle. If passed, it would guarantee patients more access and more care. It would expand choice and protect people from HMOs by holding HMOs accountable for bad decisions regarding patient care.

I support the Patients' Bill of Rights, but I don't believe we have gone far enough to ensure that every citizen in America is guaranteed health care. We live in a technology era when it is quite possible to provide every citizen with a national health care plan. It should be a right, not a privilege, to be healthy in America.

If Denmark, Sweden, and even Canada can have national health coverage for their citizens, why, in the greatest nation in the world, can't we? Because our government is more interested in protecting the rights and dollars of big business than those of its own people. We should not have a situation where only people at a certain economic level can afford to be healthy. We should be able to guarantee health through public hospitals.

We need to eliminate those HMOs and those in the health care racket who use money, instead of sound care, as a determining factor for who gets to be healthy in this country. It's a shame that the people at the bottom, who are poor, are living in a nation that could see them well but would rather have people make money selling health than provide health to all of its citizens.

And now they're talking about cloning. I personally have moral questions about our cloning anything and playing God. But I certainly don't see why government ought to invest in this. What is really the end goal? Until we democratize health care in this country, we can't even begin to talk about cloning.

If you can't provide people with the most basic health care, how can we be sure that those organs derived from cloning will ever be for anyone but the wealthy? Is cloning to provide healthy organs for everybody or just the wealthy? Are we again going to use public dollars to take care of a billionaire who needs a new liver when we don't want to give the average American cough syrup? I'm not going to be naive enough to think that everyone will have a chance to benefit from the cloning of humans for organ use, especially given our system's current health care policies.

A recent study conducted by the Institute of Medicine found that racial and ethnic minorities in this country receive lower-quality health care than whites—even when their insurance and income are the same. And I'm to believe that if allowed to clone, this country will be fair in providing care and organs to those who need it?

Look at how this government has responded to the AIDS epidemic. While millions are suffering from HIV in this country and while AIDS has become the number-one killer of blacks between the ages of twenty-five and forty-four, finding a cure or even finding some relief from this devastating disease has been all but met with a yawn by this government. It's as if Acquired Immune Deficiency Syndrome has left our national consciousness. Why? Because AIDS mainly affects the poor, the Latino, the black.

One in 50 black men and one in 160 black women are HIV-positive—compared to one in 250 and one in 3,000 white men and women. The U.S. Centers for Disease Control and Prevention in Atlanta estimates that almost 60 percent of all new HIV infections are occurring among blacks. And in Africa, every twenty-five seconds a person is infected with AIDS.

I think that there must be a real commitment to fight AIDS and to fight it in a way that would not be limited and narrow but rather geared toward solving the problem. That would include improving drug relief programs, relaxing certain patterns that stand in the way of servicing people. When you have people dying by the hundreds of thousands, it seems to me to be inhumane—and certainly immoral—to hold up relief on a business pattern or on some technical, legal quirk that stops them from getting drug relief. If it weren't Africa but somewhere else, would the world really stand by and allow hundreds of thousands of other kinds of people to die like that while we are arguing about some patent or whether some drug company filled out a form right? If AIDS were killing white Americans in the numbers it is killing blacks and Latinos, would the government drag its feet the way it has been? It seems to me to be so bizarre that we would even have this debate, given the gravity of the epidemic.

Perhaps another reason why there hasn't been such a big push to expedite new drug patents that may cure or slow down HIV is because AIDS is still deemed to be a "gay" disease. Our sense of homophobia overwhelms our sense of moral compassion for people who need us to fight for the research and whatever else is necessary to get our arms around this dreaded disease. I think that in the end, God will not be kind or merciful to those who ignored—based on some sense of taboo—something that we should have highlighted and that we could have cured.

As a minister, I am particularly disturbed by those who have wrapped themselves in the cloth while throwing judgment on their fellow man. I have heard ministers claim that AIDS is a curse from God for the homosexual and the immoral.

If God set aside this curse of AIDS for homosexuals, then why doesn't God have curses for other sins? I am taught that there is no one sin greater than another. To the same ministers that I've heard say that AIDS is a curse for homosexuality, I will ask them, "Well, where is the curse for your adultery? Or the curse for your gambling? Or the curse for your lying? Or the curse for misusing the church's money?" I think their position absolutely is grounded in their own bias.

God is not a vindictive God who targets certain sins. And for us to reduce God to our own convenient tormentor of what we do not like or what we feel is a particularly bad sin, is abominable. We, who call ourselves leaders—both moral and political—must be willing to serve all people. We cannot divide this land into the haves and the have nots, the sinners and the saints. Because there but for the grace of God, go I.

AIDS and HIV Plan:

1. Free AIDS testing available on demand

2. Government drug subsidy for the low-income, HIV-positive uninsured

3. Federal research-and-development funds for drug

companies tied to their voluntary provision of lower-cost drugs to the low-income underinsured and to their provision of lower-cost drugs for developing countries

4. Federal funding for sex education and for public relations campaigns supporting abstinence and contraception

5. Substance-abuse treatment on demand (in prisons as well)

CHAPTER ELEVEN

★

VOTING AND CAMPAIGN REFORM

In November 2000, I went to Florida on the heels of the voting debacle. Our reports showed that tens of thousands of votes—primarily in black and Jewish areas—were not counted or were not accounted for properly. I went to Florida to investigate.

When I arrived in West Palm Beach, while they were still doing the count, I got out of the car and there were about forty to fifty white Republicans waiting for me. They went crazy and started heckling me. I couldn't believe it. I said to them, "You guys call yourselves patriots but have the audacity to be out here trying to stop counting the votes of the people?"

I'll never forget that morning in West Palm Beach. While I was outside the voting center interviewing upset and disenfranchised voters, one of the hecklers yelled out, "Al, why don't you just get over it?"

"Get over it?!" I said. "It might be easy for you to get over it, because all you had to do was turn eighteen to be able to vote.

During my lifetime, my people did not have the right to vote. My mother could not vote until she was well into her forties. And I will die fighting before I "just get over it" and allow it to go back to the days of Jim Crow.

Get over it?

I can't, especially when I think of how those poor girls were killed in that church in Birmingham one Sunday morning during Sunday school—and they weren't bothering anybody, weren't even in the movement; they just went to church that morning and lost their lives. Those four little girls were like my daughters. I can't get over it.

When I think of Medgar Evers who was in his thirties, with three kids in the house, and who got out of his car one night and, in his own driveway in Mississippi, got his brains blown out because he was leading a voter rights campaign, I can't get over it. Medgar Evers never got to see any of his children become adults, didn't know if they married or went to college. He just died to give me the right to vote.

When I think of how two Jews and a black man—Andy Goodman, Michael Schwerner, and James Chaney—left the Northeast in June 1964 to make sure that I would have the right to vote, and never returned home, I'm never going to get over that. And I'm never going to stop until we are sure that those people didn't pay that price for nothing.

Too many people died, too many people spent cold nights in jail, too many pregnant women had dogs bite their stomachs, for us to get over it, for us to sit back and do nothing.

The most shocking and baffling development to come out of the November 2000 elections was how easily the Democratic Party—the so-called party of the people—gave up. I feel that the biggest letdown—and I don't think *betrayal* is too strong a word—is that the Democrats threw in the towel on protecting voting rights in Florida. We played it totally partisan and did not deal with the constitutional law.

I had to do something. In Florida, we retained attorney Jesse McCrary, the first black to be secretary of state of Florida. (He was elected, unlike Secretary Katherine Harris, who was appointed after the laws were changed). We filed the first-ever voter rights lawsuit in that state.

Nationally, we cannot wait until 2004 to have a repeat of 2000. In 2001, Congressman John Conyers and Senator Christopher Dodd introduced the Equal Protection of Voting Rights Act in response to the debacle that was the 2000 Elections. The Dodd-Conyers election reform would make the voting apparatus uniform throughout the country—we would have the same kind of voting machinery everywhere. It would also allow all voters to verify correctness of their ballots before casting them, and it would make sure that registered voters whose names do not appear on voter registration lists are able to vote and the legitimacy of their vote should be verified later. The bill also calls for voters to receive a sample ballot and voting instructions before Election Day. I support the Dodd-Conyers reform package. We must have a national voting system that is the same everywhere. If you can take somebody who received their driver's license in Nevada and pull it up in New York, why can't we do that with voting? If we can automate and standardize banking, why can't we have a national standard by which we vote? Why can't we bring the voting process into the twenty-first century, into the technology era—bring voters into the new technology era?

As we approach the next presidential election, it is paramount that we institute standard voting procedures all over the country. There is no reason why we shouldn't have federal standards for voting. If we pride ourselves on being a great democracy, as the pinnacle of democracy for the world, why do we have not only different voting procedures in different states, but also different procedures in different counties in the same state? In Florida, Dade County had one way of counting votes, Broward County had another, and there was yet another in Palm Beach. One county used hanging chads; another used pregnant chads; another used an automated system like an ATM.

What happened in November 2000 was not only ridiculous and a miscarriage of justice, but it also undermined the very electoral procedure that defines this democracy. When I was in Florida, I met a man from Tallahassee who had been voting for twenty-six years. He told me he could not vote in the 2000 Elections because they told him he needed three picture IDs. He didn't have three picture IDs. Three picture IDs? Most people have only two, if that—a license and a passport. Why did he need three to vote? This was a man who had voted successfully for twenty-six years; why the new rules? This was clearly set up to stifle certain voters and keep them from casting their ballot. It's absolutely absurd. Anytime you have different laws at different places you open the possibility for injustice. A captain at the voting precinct can have the power to create any rules he or she wants, because there's no one standard in place to enforce.

There must be a national standard. Anytime you can write a check in New Mexico and it can clear in hours in Massachusetts, but your vote cannot be clearly counted, there is a serious problem. And the problem is power. People in power want to manipulate the vote to keep themselves in office. They talk about reform, but they don't really want it. It doesn't work in their favor. The incumbents in Congress and the Senate do not want to make voting easier, because the more democracy works, the more accountable they will be. They would actually prefer to suppress the vote.

In many black communities when we start voter registration, I've had some of the local incumbents say, "Don't do that!" Only 4,000–5,000 people may vote in the primary, and those are the folks they are sure of. If we bring out 10,000 more people who may not like what's going on in their neighborhood, that incumbent may not win.

How can you on the one hand talk about voters rights and on the other hand not guarantee that the vote is not in any way minimized or suppressed in the name of keeping your fiefdom in South Central L.A. or Oklahoma City or wherever?

And after we reform the election process, it's time we revisit who actually gets to vote. I believe it is inhumane and hypocritical for a convicted felon who served his or her time and successfully got off parole to have their right to vote permanently revoked. It runs counter to the whole notion of a person paying one's debt to society. The idea of reformation is to reform a person to be a productive citizen of society. You cannot tell those persons that you want them to be productive citizens but then tell them they will not have the right to participate as full citizens. Why tell them they've done their time, they've paid their debt to society, when they can no longer participate in society, forever? Under this system, you're not giving them a chance to rehabilitate. You're giving them a sentence within a sentence—and a life sentence from democracy. That is simply another way of suppressing the vote.

The right to vote and the right to have every person's vote counted is near and dear to my heart. That's why I go into churches, community centers, and even on the street corners, subways, and urban centers to get people to register. You have to go where the people are. And more importantly, you have to give them a reason to vote.

The times I've run for office, I've been able to bring out a large vote—especially new voters, because people will vote if they feel they have someone to vote for who speaks for them. But their vote must not be circumvented by the process. The problem we have is that most politicians aren't speaking for people. People don't answer the phone unless it's ringing. They say, "If you're not talking to me, why should I come out and vote for you?"

What November 2000 did was make the people question the system, and give them even less of a reason to come out to cast their vote. It made folks think, "Why bother? I will just stay home." No democracy can afford that.

Here is my ten-point plan on both Election Reform and how finances ought to be used and not used in political campaigns.

Election and Campaign Finance Reform Plans:

1. Multipartisan commission to create a national standard for voting booths, paid for by tax return check-off

2. National standard for eligibility for federal election participation (identification requirements, etc.)

3. Stiffer federal penalties for impeding voting rights (federal law and jail time)

4. Public financing of all federal campaigns, paid for by tax return check-off

5. Limit the amount of money any individual can spend on his or her own campaign to the median income of a family of four (roughly, $35,000)

6. Eliminate issue and attack ads in the last three weeks of campaign:

We pollute the political process when we trivialize politics as if we were selling a product. The attack ads don't deal with substantive issues, and Americans should make their choices based on issues and policies, not based on the lies of some spin doctor or some hired attack dog.

7. Increase disclosure rules so that all contact with donors subsequent to contribution is published (enforce this by stricter penalties for false reporting)

8. Reduce annual total amount of campaign contributions to whichever is the larger figure:

(a) one percent of annual take-home median income of a family of four (roughly, $280)

(b) the median amount of a monthly social security check (roughly, $300)

9. Allow donations only to those candidates an individual is eligible to vote for during the upcoming general election (thereby limiting individuals to donate to a handful of candidates a year)

10. Constitutional Amendment: "The right of legal residents of the United States to vote shall not be denied or abridged by the United States or by any state on account of age, citizenry, or prison record." (This dramatically expands the number of blacks, Hispanics, and students eligible to vote)

CHAPTER TWELVE

★

THE WAR ON
DRUGS & CRIMINAL
JUSTICE REFORM

Early in my career, I spent a lot of time in the ghetto fighting drug dealers. I watched crack and heroin totally
devastate families and whole neighborhoods. I watched
women do crazy things for drugs, even cause harm to their
own children.

But as I got more into this battle against drugs, I realized
I was on the wrong side. America is on the wrong side of
this drug fight. Nancy Reagan headed up a campaign
against drugs where she called for kids to "Just Say No."
The government needs to heed those words and just say
no—no to planes and ships carrying drugs to our shores, no
to drug governments abroad that we are in cahoots with.

We have concentrated the war on drugs on the wrong
side. We have targeted the dealer at the end of the line in-

stead of the supplier at the beginning of the line. We are not going after those countries who openly allow drug trade.

In response to the attack on September 11, we bombed caves in Afghanistan. But we didn't bomb poppy fields that make the drugs that put heroin onto the streets of South Central L.A. and Harlem. The priority seems to be to lock up the low-level guys, many under federal mandatory drug sentencing laws who are caught with a small quantity of crack. Now, I don't condone the actions of that guy, but why should he spend a minimum of five to ten years in jail for a small quantity of crack the size of a "Sweet 'N Low" packet, while the drug lord doesn't face any mandatory time? There's something wrong with that picture.

I supported the Rockefeller drug laws following the death of Len Bias. Something had to be done. But in hindsight, it was the wrong answer. To give someone mandatory time, no matter the circumstances, with no parole, while someone caught with a hundred pounds of loose cocaine gets no mandatory time and parole, is screwy. It doesn't make sense.

Now, almost twenty years later after the passing of the Rockefeller laws, we have become victimized by the disparity. And now you have guys who are coming home—the first generation to face this—from five-to-ten-year mandatory time, who only went to jail for that little bag of crack in their pocket. And they're coming home to no jobs, no training programs, no structure to absorb them, and no way to reintroduce them into the community. These guys are candidates for the first crime they can commit to go back. And some of them want to go back.

I've talked to guys on the corner who tell me that at least in jail they're promised three meals a day, it's warm in the winter, and they have air conditioning in the summertime. There's no guarantee of any of that out on the streets.

It's a sad society when in some communities, jail is a step up—particularly a society as wealthy as this one. The war on drugs must be fought at a higher level. We have to use trade leverage to go after the countries that produce the drugs—who openly allow drugs to be in their economy—and put them out of business.

And this country has a very poor history of doing that.

Perhaps the reason why the United States doesn't go after the real drug lords and the real drug producers and sellers is because it would be bad for business on both ends. We make money with the countries that produce the drugs, and we make money by sending the low-level drug criminal to jail for a long time.

I am equally opposed to the three-strikes-and-you're-out law that came under the Democrats, for the same reason why I oppose the Rockefeller Drug Laws. Instead of setting up a multitiered way to permanently incarcerate people, we ought to be setting up programs that will prevent people from becoming repeat offenders. What the Crime Bill of the Clinton Administration did was spend more money to penalize and incarcerate people than on having things like afterschool programs, prenatal care, and tutorial programs

that would prevent young people from becoming repeat offenders. They didn't give any alternative to crime. I think
that we have become far too much a society that is bent on
punishing people rather than correcting behavior.

When I was growing up, they used to call them "correctional institutions." Now they are called "detention centers."
The change of names shows a change of philosophy. We no
longer look to "correct" behavior; we simply look to detain
or lock folks up. Why do we detain them? It creates jobs in
suburban areas. It provides a low-wage or no-wage labor
source to make things.

Prisons also are making many vendors wealthy, from
those who provide the steel and materials for cells, to the
people who provide the food, to the folks who do the laundry. When I had to do those ninety days at the Brooklyn
Detention Center, I sat around my cell and wondered, "Who's
got the toilet tissue contract here?" and "Who provides the
soap?" I had clean underwear every day. And I wondered
how much the people got who supplied the prison with
laundry detergent. All of these services are million-dollar
contracts, multimillion-dollar government contracts. And
the more jails, the more these people make. No one looks at
these budgets. Imagine the soap contract. Imagine the detergent contract; imagine the food contract—with three
square meals a day for each inmate. Imagine the sneaker
contract. You could make a billion dollars off the uniform
contract alone. More than 50 percent of the inmates are

black and Latino, and I bet very few of those government contracts are going to blacks and Latinos.

We are dealing with a prison-industrial complex. Prisons are big business. It's certainly not in the best interest of those who run the prisons who are using inmate labor—cheap and in some cases free labor that supplies everything from license plates to jeans to furniture—to reform criminals. It is in their interest to detain people and get as many detainees as possible. Don't dare reform a criminal. That's bad for business. If you reform too many, then we will not be able to build more jails, and prison industrialists won't make their money or get their contracts.

There are more than two million people in jail in the United States—more than in any civilized society in the world. How are other societies that do not have our wealth, that don't have our advanced culture, that don't have our education, able to have a prison system that leads to corrective behavior while we have more people locked up than anyone in the civilized world?

And who is getting locked up the most? Blacks and Latinos. A coincidence? Absolutely not. I've had some racists say that the reason why the jails are full of blacks and Latinos is because they commit more crimes. But that's simply not true. The truth is, whites who commit the same crimes as blacks and Latinos are more likely to walk. Blacks and Latinos are targeted more for crimes. Racial profiling is real. If you stop more blacks and Latinos, you will naturally have more arrests of blacks and Latinos. And studies show that if you are poor, you have an even greater chance of going to jail.

So in the United States, according to studies, if you're black or Hispanic you're four times more likely to get jail time than your white counterpart. That's not justice. That's "just us."

Criminal Justice Reform Plan:

1. Laws must be based on what's right, not based on the economics of the person arrested.

2. We need real leaders in this field, not politicians. We're talking about people's lives, not political chips or pawns.

3. We must put judges on the benches who show sensitivity in dealing with all types of people and who will not act out their biases and bigotry. We must depoliticize the judiciary. We have to call for an electoral process for the judiciary. I think a lot of these judges need to be elected on a federal level, where they are accountable to the people.

4. The jury selection process must change. In many areas, juries are selected from voting rolls, but in some areas it goes by newspaper subscriptions. So if you live in New York, they may use the subscription list

from the *New York Times*. That's absurd. That's not a jury of your peers. Juries must reflect the demographics of the area that you live in.

5. Any public servant accused of a crime must always face a jury trial. Firemen, policemen, or any politician should not be given the option of a trial by judge if they are prosecuted for something on the job. If you are doing a public service or commit a crime doing a public service, you should have to face the public. Let the public vindicate you, because that's who you are working for.

Chapter Thirteen

★

EDUCATION

We are supposedly in the technological age. America is among the world leaders in technology and science. How is it possible, in a country so rich in resources, that our children are so far behind in education? There is no excuse for ignorance to exist in America. It is impossible for people to compete or survive with the technocracy in America without education and information. Public education must be our number-one priority. Without a successful system to educate our children, we are doomed.

The key to ensuring success is to make sure that we have people who can deliver the product to students. That means investing in quality and in qualified teachers. I would pay teachers more money in order to attract better teachers, and institute merit pay to reward those who are getting the job done.

There have been many who have suggested abolishing local school boards throughout the nation and giving control to the mayor of that city. In New York that debate has been brewing for years. I would not be in favor of abolishing community control. The idea of everything being controlled by the mayor in a major city like New York is not good. I think that instead of eliminating community boards, we should put more energy into perfecting the school board system and eliminating corruption and mismanagement. We have not perfected community control.

Certainly, parental participation in the elections of local school boards has been very low. But I don't see that as apathy or the parents' not caring, as much as that the boards have not given them a reason to vote and be involved. Many just feel helpless. But even if the lack of participation is parental apathy, it doesn't justify not trying to make the system work. You don't throw the baby out with the bath water.

Schools should have maximum options for participation by the community and parents. Abolishing the board of education in favor of mayoral control does not fix the system. In fact, I believe it opens the system to even more political patronage and would lead to the possibility of further corruption of the system. The power in the hands of one, or absolute power, corrupts absolutely.

The public school system across the country is far from perfect. And we certainly need reform. But let's reform decentralization. Let's perfect it, not eliminate it. You have to balance the power in the schools between the community, the city council, and the mayor. You have to build a three-tier system—not unlike our very government with the executive, judicial, and legislative branches—where each can check the other. Let's democratize the process. Let's perfect the process.

And vouchers are not the answer, either. There has been a widespread movement across the nation to institute vouchers as a means to give a few children a chance to escape the public school system by using public dollars to allow them to go to private or parochial schools. The problem with vouchers is that they don't service everybody. The nature of the voucher argument is that we can only take care of a small percentage of the children. I think that the emphasis has to be on educating everyone. Vouchers at its best can only service about 10 percent of the students. So are we consigning the other 90 percent to failure? They aren't going to get a good education? The role of government should never be to aim toward taking care of 10 percent of the population.

And I feel the same way about charter schools. While competition does breed excellence in most quarters, in education, taking public dollars away from public schools and putting them into a private system will again only serve a few. And it's not good enough to have a few children get an education while the rest suffer. We must find a way to fix the system so that every child's need is serviced through the public school system. That's reform.

Ultimately, however, if reform or real change is going to take place in our public schools, it has to also take place in our homes. All of the responsibility to educate our children cannot simply fall on government. Parents have to step up and ensure that their children are getting a proper education.

In the segregated South under Jim Crow, where schools were separate and unequal, blacks received a better education than they are getting today. The importance of education in a black home was stressed by parents, who knew the power of education. Teachers lived in the same community as the children and attended the same churches. There was accountability there. Education was a community-based effort. We had more of an input with what was going on in the schools. We felt that we had more of a personal and hands-on type of access. I think that we—parents, particularly black parents—have got to blame ourselves for that.

I'm not at all calling for segregation to return, but parents must have the attitude that they will not accept failure from the system or from their children. We have taken too much responsibility from the home and put too much on the schools. We should have never consigned our children to the system.

It's like when, after decentralization, parents said, "Okay, we have community control; now we can relax and let the system educate our children." That simply cannot work. Now that we have some community control, parents have the opportunity to be involved even more in the system, not less. I know many of us work and are busy. But we should never be too busy to know what's happening with our children.

I go to my children's Open School Week and I try to make a few Parent-Teacher Association meetings. And I always get these curious looks. People are amazed that I'm there. I met with my children's teachers, and even they said they were surprised that someone so "busy" would be there. My children weren't surprised that I was there, because they know how important their education is to me. I let them know. But the teachers and others parents were surprised. They ought to be more surprised if someone like me *doesn't* have the time to visit my children's school. I think there is a certain responsibility that we are missing that we need to publicly condemn. The system has failed, but a lot of the system's failing is because we have failed our kids. The system picked up on the fact that parents don't care, so why should they. And that has to change.

Education Plan:

1. Full funding of Head Start

2. Fund Pell Grants at originally intended levels

3. Full funding of Title One:

Title One was established to give every child a solid education, and all educational facilities are to receive government money. But until we have full funding and a real government position on where we are going to put real dollars behind our advocacy of giving everyone a chance to learn, leaving no one behind, our education system will forever be in trouble. The Bible says, "Where a man's treasure lies, so does his heart." George Bush cannot say he's the education president and not fund Title One. This cannot be the age of education in Congress if our funding reflects something different. It's time for government to put its money where its mouth is.

4. Support for civil rights litigation about quality of schools (line-item funding and authorization of such geared to Legal Services Corporation)

5. Public school choice

6. Increased funding for bilingual education (to build support among Hispanic communities)

7. Support of policies ending property-tax funding of public schools:

Money spent in underprivileged areas per student is supposed to be the same as the per-student expenditures in affluent areas. But where property taxes are higher—basically in residential and suburban areas—those schools receive a better quality of education and better books, and there is a better environment for learning. If we continue to tie property taxes to public school funding, we will continue to have an unequal system. Therefore, if the funding is based on inheriting that setup, inner-city young people will continue to get less money.

8. Interest-free student loan deferment for students who provide services such as teaching, social work, medicine, etc., to underserved communities during their term of service

9. Student Loan repayment reform—creating progressive interest payments, whereby lower-income graduates pay lower interest rates and higher-income students pay higher interest rates

10. Educational empowerment zones

11. Volunteerism encouragement—federal funding for a community teachers' program, wherein local experts are trained to be part-time teachers in public schools

12. Education Constitutional Amendment—"The right of equal access to any elementary or secondary school receiving public funding shall not be abridged."

(This creates public school choice with transportation covered by the state and protects schools from cherry-picking provisions should vouchers ever become law.

Chapter Fourteen

★

The Military

The history of black soldiers is a sad and painful one. There is no American war that has happened in the history of this country that black soldiers did not fight in. Crispus Attucks—a fugitive slave, a black man—was working on a dock when Samuel Adams put forth the call for men to fight against the British troops. Attucks answered the call, and he made history as the first person to die in the famed Boston massacre, which officially kicked off the Revolutionary War.

Even when black people were constitutionally considered three-fifths a man, we were full men on the battlefield for this country. When we had no rights, we always had the right to fight for this country.

The humiliation of going to foreign shores and coming

home and seeing the people they fought against walking past them into restaurants that served "whites only," or watching the "enemy" be allowed to drink from a water fountain or relieve themselves in a toilet that by law they could not use, is what our grandfathers had to suffer. It made them stronger, but it is also a despicable part of history that America does not want to come to terms with.

So as we enter yet another war—a war on terror—black men and women must reflect on their curious history in this country and demand that no longer will they fight on the front lines abroad and be treated as second-class citizens at home.

We cannot send our sons and daughters off to war while we still have a disparity in health care, education, and the criminal justice system here at home. Yet we still have a disproportionate number of people of color in the military. If Bush invades Iraq, as it is said he is planning to do in early 2003, there will be a disproportionate number of military personnel who will come from communities that get less education and less health care, and who find it more difficult to get a mortgage. So even if the disparity is not as blatant as it was for our grandfathers, there is still the blatant gap between the money we invest in the military and the results we get out of America. Again, the trickle-down theory doesn't work here.

Even before September 11, the Bush Administration was increasing the military budget. And since September 11, Bush has presented Congress with a $2.1 trillion wartime budget for 2003—the majority of which would go toward funding the military. At the same time, he has called for limiting spending in domestic areas. That means we're building a bigger and better military to fight abroad and protect home. The problem with this mentality is, what are we protecting at home? We are shortchanging education and other social programs. We are asking our men and women to fight on foreign soils and not guaranteeing that they will have something worthwhile to come home to.

And of the trillions of dollars being poured into the military, very little of that is getting to those people who are actually fighting. The soldiers have not seen a dramatic increase in salaries and service. No, that money is fattening the pockets of the fat cats and contractors who service the military. There is a lot of administrative overage. You have more fat in the military budget than probably any budget in the United States government.

So on one hand you see this huge increase in military spending last year, but on the other hand, that money didn't make its way to the soldiers. It went to the bureaucracy— this coming from the people who claim to be about small government. They are the ones who are supposed to be against bureaucracy and big government. And they are, when it comes to providing aid to social programs and helping the poor. But they want huge government when it comes to the military-industrial complex.

I want to know how these huge budgets keep America safe. And how did America become so vulnerable with all these people getting all this money? And why isn't America safe today?

Don't get me wrong; I am not anti-military, nor would I recommend that people not serve and fight for our country. I'm just saying we need to take a second look at how we're handling the military. And we need to create an even playing field at home before we go out and try to straighten out the world's problems.

Yes, we must have the capacity to protect American citizens and America's shores. But I think that we should always use military action as the last resort.

We have seen the elimination of Russia as a superpower, leaving only one superpower on the globe. And given the financial standing and the military superiority of our country, we don't have to use what everyone else knows we have. We do not have to play bully all the time. There's an old adage that says the more power you accumulate, the softer you can speak. America can whisper and be even more effective.

I think that those who are still barking like we are in the middle of a cold war rather than understanding the new setup of the world only exacerbate problems rather than resolve them.

So as military leader I would maintain a strong military. I would maintain an able and well-equipped Army, Navy, Air Force, and Marine Corps. But I would not use them unless they are absolutely necessary. I would have them built up and maintained for defensive measures, not offensive measures. And I would eliminate a lot of the fat in the military budget. A lot of what is in the military budget, particularly in this administration, goes to perks and goes to feed military corporate contracts. Not enough of that money goes toward defending the American people.

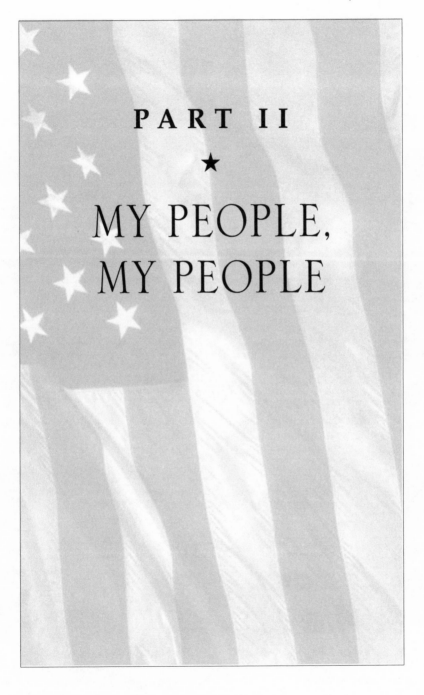

PART II

★

MY PEOPLE, MY PEOPLE

★

CHAPTER FIFTEEN

KINGMAKER? NEW YORK'S 2001 MAYOR'S RACE

Early in 2000 the mayoral sweepstakes began. There was talk of my running for mayor. These talks were legitimate because I had run four years before and came within a fraction of causing a runoff against Ruth Messinger in the primaries. It would have been the first mayoral runoff in New York City in twenty years.

All of the contenders—Mark Green, Alan Hevesi, Fernando Ferrer, and Peter Vallone—were 1) trying to convince me not to run, and 2) trying to convince me to support them.

I had several meetings with all of them. Alan Roskoff, a friend of mine, was working on the Green campaign. Roskoff supported me when I ran for the United States Senate and he was also a big supporter during my first run for mayor. He wanted me to hook up with Green. We had dinner together, and then Green came to the House of Justice two or three times.

One day, Roskoff calls me and says, "Mark wants to go out, just you and him and your wives." I said, "All right."

There was a new Broadway play opening about the Holocaust. So I had to convince Kathy to go. She usually doesn't like to get involved in politics, but I got her to go this time. That night we pulled up to the theater and walked right into cameras. The next day, it's all in the major newspapers. After the play, we walked from the theater to Sardi's, and the four of us had dinner. Green spent most of the night talking about why I should support him for mayor.

By this time it's early 2001, and we had the first mayoral debate with all of the candidates at the House of Justice for Martin Luther King Day. I had, by that time, decided I would not run for mayor, and I was beginning to think about whom I would support.

It had come down to Green, who had a pretty decent record as a liberal, and Freddy Ferrer, who—to me—had a pretty decent record overall. Hevesi and I had a hostile background, and even though we had kind of made up, I was not going to support him. And Peter Vallone and I were cordial but we didn't agree on a lot of issues.

It got down to late Spring of 2001, and I was still debating about whom I would endorse. Green and I had dinner again, just us, and we talked about how he understood what I was going through with Jesse Jackson. Green was a protégé of Ralph Nader and at times was struggling with him over issues.

It's interesting to note that during the 2000 presidential elections, when Green and I first started talking, Green brought up that Ralph Nader could not get into Harlem and he didn't think it was fair.

"Now I'm not supporting my mentor for president, because I'm a Democrat with Al Gore, but I think he should have an opportunity to be heard," Green said.

I said, "You're right." And I invited Ralph Nader to the House of Justice to speak. It was Mark Green who made that possible.

After my last dinner with Green, I still had not made up my mind. On the next Saturday, I was driving up the FDR Drive in Manhattan, heading to the House of Justice to do my weekly radio broadcast, when I heard on the radio that Robert Kennedy Jr. and Dennis Rivera were arrested for protesting in Vieques.

A couple of years before, Ruben Berrios, an activist from Vieques, spoke at the House of Justice, and I said publicly then that if they started bombing again, I would go down there and protest. Many in the Puerto Rican community had stood with me and went to jail with me during our protests against the police shooting of Amadou Diallo, and I made a personal commitment to them. They showed real unity with us; we should stand with them. Before I got to the office, I called Roberto Ramirez on my cell phone.

"Roberto, I heard they just arrested Kennedy and Dennis in Vieques; we need to go down and do this like we did the Diallo protests," I said. What made the Diallo protests so effective is that every day we would have people down at One Police Plaza getting arrested. It was the consistency of the numbers that made an impact, and I felt we could do the same in Vieques.

"If we can't do it every day like Diallo, then every other day someone needs to go down there and protest," I said. "We have to keep the pressure on. We need to keep people going to jail, and I'm willing to do that."

He said, "You are?!"

"Yeah," I said.

"When do you want to go?"

"Let's go now," I said. "You want to do it so there's continuity. You have to back up the arrest of Kennedy and Dennis quickly."

He called me back and said, "We can't go today; let's go Monday." I said okay. I did my broadcast and prepared to leave for Vieques.

On Monday, we head off to Puerto Rico. Roberto brings Assemblyman Jose Rivera and Adolpho Carrion, who is now Bronx Borough president. We go over to the bombing site, climb through the fence, protest, and get arrested. We all go to jail.

The whole time we're in jail, Roberto is in my ear about endorsing Freddy.

"We need a coalition, that's why you should go for Freddy for mayor," he said.

"I don't know," I said. "It's between Mark and Freddy."

When I get back from Vieques, former mayor David Dinkins was in my ear about supporting Mark Green. Just about everybody was for Mark Green. Just about the only person pushing Freddy—besides the Latinos—was Bill Lynch. But everyone else was either with Green or someone else. Then I got a call from Percy Sutton, who said he was going with Freddy. "That this is the future and we need to move forward," he said.

In my office, there were people supporting different people. On the board of the National Action Network, it was the same thing. There was no real consensus. And there were even some pushing me to run.

In late May, I was doing a segment on CNN and I got a cell phone call while I was in the studio. My secretary said the lawyer called and said I am supposed to be at a hearing tomorrow in Puerto Rico. I said, "A hearing? A hearing about what?! There's no way I can get to Puerto Rico by tomorrow. Get a delay."

She was adamant that the lawyer said we had to be there. She connected me to the attorney. He said, "This judge is crazy. He's not going to bend. I think we can beat this, but you have to show up."

"I don't think I can get there," I said.

"You have got to get there; this guy is not playing," he said.

Roberto calls and says we better go because this judge will put out a federal warrant for us. I'm at the Plaza Hotel by now, eating lunch with Eddie Harris, who heads up the communication and film arm of the Network. I said to Roberto, "I have to run home and get some clothes and I will meet you at the airport."

I go home, get some clothes, and head out to Kennedy Airport. While driving there, I get a call from Sanford Rubenstein, the attorney who handled the Abner Louima case and who worked with us on other cases, as well. We needed to meet on a police brutality case. We were also collecting data on whether I should run for president, and he was heading up my exploratory team. I told Sanford Rubenstein to meet me at the airport and we could talk there.

"You have money; why don't you just buy a ticket to Puerto Rico and we can talk on the plane ride there?" I told him.

All the way down, Sanford and I are talking presidential stuff. We get to the courthouse and find out we're actually on trial. There were forty people on trial for civil disobedience in Vieques. The guy representing us in Vieques approaches the bench and says, "Your honor, I was only hired to arraign them. I'm not supposed to argue their case." The judge said, "I don't care; we're doing this trial now."

"Wait a minute; they have their lawyer here," our guy says. "Can he have time to prepare the case?"

The judge said no. "We're going now!"

And the prosecutor put on the witnesses from the Navy who said we did go through the fence. And that was it. The judge said, "Okay, guilty! Get ready for sentencing."

After he said, "Guilty," I said, "Wait a minute, Your Honor, can we get at least a ten-minute break?" The judge granted it. We went into the hall and I said to Roberto and the rest of them, "This guy is going to put us in jail. This is an old-fashioned railroading." And I know about railroading. Roberto and the others had never been through anything like this. But I knew.

"Are you serious?" they said.

"I'm telling you, we may get bailed out, but this guy is definitely putting us in jail," I said.

So I took off my ring and watch and gave them to Eddie Harris, who'd traveled with us, and I suggested that Roberto and Adolpho and Jose do the same. I told Sanford Rubenstein to find us a bail bondsman, and we headed back into the courtroom for the sentencing.

The judge says, "Sharpton and Garcia (another guy who had done this three or four times before), over there." He pointed to a separate area of the court. I knew then that I was going to get more time than the rest of them—me and whoever Garcia was.

"Ramirez, Rivera, and Carrion"—and he rattled off the other thirty or so names—"thirty days!" the judge started.

"Garcia, you've done this before, and Sharpton, you've done this before in the States—ninety days!"

Ninety days! I couldn't believe it. I was supposed to renew my wedding vows in two weeks. So the lawyer asked if I could start my sentence after that. The judge said no.

"Take them away, now!" he said.

"But, Your Honor . . ."

"Take them away, now!"

They put the leg shackles and the handcuffs on us and took us away. I looked at Roberto Ramirez and said, "Don't worry. It's just like Bull Connor. He just made your case for you."

"What are you talking about?" he said.

"Anytime they act this irrationally, it only helps your cause. Now, it's going to cost us some time in jail. But it's going to make the case."

When we got out to go to the police van, I looked up and saw all the cameras across the yard. I told Roberto and the others, "When you get out there, walk real slow. They need to see how they have us in leg irons for a nonviolent protest." And sure enough, the next day that was the picture all over the world—of them taking us out to the wagon. At the time, I expected to get bailed out. But the judge said no bail.

That first night, they had all of the Vieques protestors— about forty of us—together in our own compartment in the federal jail. In our section, they started having a rally in honor of me. I was the only non-Latino in jail, and they wanted to thank me for coming there and helping to revitalize the issue of the military bombings in Vieques. It was real nice camaraderie that night. And every hour, it seemed, I was getting a phone call.

Congressman Charles Rangel, Congressman Jose Serrano, Senator Chuck Schumer—all of New York's federal officials were trying to get us out. But it seemed hopeless with that judge, and I'm thinking, "I'm going to have to do ninety days in Puerto Rico away from my family and everybody."

I tried not to focus on that, and I got Roberto and the others together and told them, "We should go on a hunger strike, at least for the first few days." Whenever I go to jail, I usually fast while I'm there. It helps me to focus and strengthens my resolve and my faith, and since these guys had never gone through this, I thought a fast or a hunger strike would get us on the same page.

The suggestion was met with a lukewarm response. "We'll think about it," they said.

At the jailhouse all of the guards were really supportive. They said, "Right on! You did this for the people and we're behind you." They asked if there was anything they could do for us. Roberto Ramirez said, "I'd like to make a phone call."

Jose Rivera said, "The one thing I promised Mrs. Sharpton is that Reverend Sharpton would get his chicken (everyone knows I love chicken). Can you get us some chicken?" and everyone laughed.

"What do you want, Rev?" they asked me.

"Just get me the key and I can get all the chicken I want," I said.

No one took any of it too seriously. But about an hour later, they brought in all this chicken and rice and beans. Roberto, Adolpho, and Jose looked at the chicken and then looked at me. And I said, "We can start this fast tomorrow."

At about four the next morning we hear this *boom, boom, boom!* All this noise and flashlights.

"Get up, get up!" they said. "Sharpton, Ramirez, Carrion, Rivera, get a shower and get dressed!" I know now that they must be transferring us. They shackle us again, put us in the van, and we head to the airport in San Juan at six in the morning. They can't get the tarmac door open, so they have to walk us through the airport, and people are cheering us all the way through. They empty the back of a commercial plane and put us in the back with armed United States marshals. We are on the plane, still shackled like we'd killed somebody.

When we land in New York, there are eight police cars on the tarmac at Kennedy Airport waiting for us. You would have thought we'd shot the president. They brought us to the Metropolitan Detention Center in Brooklyn, where I stayed the remaining eighty-something days.

In there, everyone from Chuck Schumer to Hillary

Clinton came to see us. And of course, the issue of the mayor's race came up on several occasions. I really had not made up my mind, even though everyone was visiting and trying to convince me to lean their way. Charlie Rangel probably visited me more than anyone else and was really pressuring me.

Over the next month, Rangel and I were going back and forth. Now, in the beginning of my career, I was no great lover of New York Representative Charles Rangel for the longest time. He'd defeated my hero, Adam Clayton Powell, for his seat in Congress.

Through the years, we became cordial but not really close. But I cannot remember a time when I would call Rangel and he wouldn't respond. We would agree or disagree on any given issue, but he was always available. In 1984, he supported Walter Mondale over Jesse Jackson, and I didn't agree with that at all. We have never really seen eye to eye politically, but here we were, talking about who *we* should support. Rangel felt we should all get behind the same person.

He wanted Dinkins, Dennis Rivera, himself, and me to have a united front—if we could all agree. I started to say that maybe we ought to do this coalition and go with Freddy (I guess being locked up and having Roberto in my ear every day was beginning to have an effect).

We wore out the conference room of the assistant warden, where they would allow us to have our visits. On one of Rangel's many visits, Roberto was in the next room having his visit. He somehow convinced the guard to let him come in and say hello to Rangel.

"Please sit down," Rangel said to Roberto. And they started talking about the relationship between blacks and Latinos in New York City and how some blacks in the Bronx felt like they didn't get a lot from Freddy and Latinos. We talked about, if there was to be a coalition, what would be expected from each side.

At the end of the day, I didn't know whether Charlie Rangel was closer or not. But I had made up my mind that I was going for Freddy. We went back to our cells—they had the four us separated on our own wing of the prison. We even had our own basketball court.

"Do you think I made progress with Charlie?" Roberto asked me.

"I don't know."

"We just got information back from the polls, and the polls say that a Dinkins endorsement will have a certain impact on the election," Roberto said. "Rangel has a certain impact, too. But the one who has the most impact is you. If you endorse Freddy, it will bring us to where we need to be."

I didn't tell him at that time that I had already made up my mind.

"Well, I'll think about it," I said.

While we're inside, Freddy, Mark Green, Hevesi, and all of them are outside marching at the jail. We get down into forty days left, and Roberto, Adolpho and Jose are out and I'm down there by myself. Roberto would come to visit. He was on my list as one of my lawyers.

I told him to get Bill Lynch on my visitors' list.

"Why?" he asked.

"Because I'm going to endorse Freddy when I get out."

"What?!" Roberto said.

"I said, I'm going with Freddy."

"Can I tell Freddy?"

"I'll tell Freddy and we'll arrange a press conference."

Bill came and I told him my plans, and that Saturday we got Freddy on the visitors' list as a family member with my wife, and I told him of my decision.

Bill wanted to tell Rangel.

"So you're going with Freddy?" Rangel asked. "Let me see what Greg Meeks [Congressman from the Sixth District] is going to do. Let's see if we can get this collective going."

"I get out in two weeks," I said. "And when I do I will make my announcement then."

The week before I got out, the assistant warden called me and told me that I had a call from Charlie Rangel.

"How you feeling, Rev?" Rangel said.

"Well, I'm still here," I said.

"Let me ask you a question. You get out the seventeenth. Why don't you let the elected officials endorse first? We get ours out and it builds up to your endorsement," Rangel said.

I said, "Fine." I had no problem with that. That afternoon Rangel and the other elected officials announced their endorsement of Freddy.

I got out at ten o'clock on the morning of August 17, 2001. Dinkins—who had already jumped the gun endorsing Mark Green—Rangel, Greg Meeks, and everyone were there when I got out. That next week, I held a press conference and announced my endorsement of Freddy. That is when Freddy got his momentum from the African-American community. And the polls showed that in the Latino community he was reinforced because a lot of grassroots Latinos, energized by our protests in Vieques, came on even stronger in support of Freddy. He even got some progressive whites.

Dennis Rivera endorsed Freddy after us. He was originally leaning toward Green before coming around to Freddy.

Right after that, Mark Green started telling people that he had never asked for my endorsement. Never asked me for my support? What was he talking about? It sounded like code to the white community. He was trying to marginalize our endorsement of Freddy and act like he didn't lose anything. I knew he was playing a race card.

He had the audacity to say on television, "I never asked Sharpton for his endorsement."

We were on New York 1 and they asked me about it. And I said, "First of all, if Mark Green wasn't seeking my endorsement, why did he take my wife and me out to Broadway and dinner? What? Were we just friends? We don't hang out. He invited me to his house for breakfast. If he didn't want my support, then what was that all about?"

Green said in response, "We were just socializing." He said he was showing himself accessible. Why would you want to socialize with someone you don't want to support you? If someone is worthy of hanging out with you, certainly they are worthy of supporting you.

"Why not just admit you played a subtle race card in Staten Island when you lied and said you never sought my endorsement?" I said to him.

Then we get the word that Herb Berman, who was running against Bill Thompson for city controller and who was on Green's ticket, was putting posters up around Brooklyn in some of the Hasidic Jewish areas that said, "A vote for Berman is a vote for . . . ," and he lists his supporters like Ed Koch and Mark Green and so on. And then the poster says, "A vote for Bill Thompson is a vote for Al Sharpton, David Dinkins, and Al Vann [councilman from Brooklyn]."

Green's people started this stuff, too. Then came the daily editorial cartoons in the *New York Post* depicting Freddy as my puppet, and Freddy handing over the keys to the city after winning, among other things.

Despite this, Freddy was still gaining in the polls. We were out there campaigning harder than ever. I think I campaigned harder for Freddy than I did for myself when *I* ran. On the morning of the primaries I was up early, campaigning in Brooklyn. I voted, made a few stops on behalf of the campaign, and then went to Junior's on Flatbush Avenue in Brooklyn for some coffee.

While there, a woman I grew up with in Washington Tillman came up to me and we were talking, and a waiter came over and said, "A plane just flew into the World Trade Center." I thought a propeller plane had got off course and it was an accident, and I went back to drinking my coffee. About twenty minutes later, I heard that another plane flew into the Trade Center.

I said, "Two planes?! Something's wrong." We got up and went to the television, and we saw that it was a terrorist attack. We tried to get to our offices, but the whole city was shut down. A sanitation worker saw us on the bridge and offered to drive me to the other side, into Manhattan. And I walked to the office and stayed there all day.

People were pouring in all day, talking about their loved ones. I called Kathy and I told her to bring the girls home from school. About eight P.M., the girls called and said they had a friend at Canaan Baptist Church whose mother worked in the World Trade Center and he hadn't heard from her. They wanted to know if he could stay with us until he found out what happened to his mother. Travis Boyd ended up staying with us for two months. His mother perished in the building.

As we were dealing with the terrorist attacks and started a counseling program at the House of Justice, we were beginning to pick up the pieces to the campaign. By now it was at fever pitch, this whole demonizing of Sharpton. The race card was being played more frequently. But we decided to stay above the fray and keep going. On Election Night, Freddy comes in number one but Green gets enough votes to force a runoff.

That last week before the runoff, there was campaigning like I had never seen—phone calls, flyers, and race-baiting. Green wins. And right away, I got a call the next day from Roberto. Green wanted to meet with us.

We meet with him and he says something to the effect of, "We need to pull the party together. I'm going to win this. But we need to be on one accord." He said he had nothing to do with a lot of the tactics of the campaign and that we should put all of that behind us.

I said, "First of all, I do not believe you didn't have anything to do with race-baiting. This could not have been done at the level it was done without your knowledge. You were too cowardly to stop it. Not only are you a coward, but you are a liar. To sit up on television and tell people you didn't ask anyone for my support is a flat-out lie."

"Al, I don't ever remember saying, 'Will you support me?'" he said.

"Yes, you did. But if you didn't, that was implicit in the dinners you took my wife and me to, the breakfast we had, and your visit to the House of Justice."

He said, "Well, I don't mind being called a coward. I don't mind being called a liar. But I do mind being called a coward *and* a liar within a five-minute period."

I said, "Well, let's try it in five seconds—you're a liar and a coward."

And that was the meeting. Mark Green and his campaign people agreed to apologize, and they would address Roberto's demands for a statewide official to denounce what happened, and if they found out who was directly responsible for the racial flyers and phone calls that they would fire them.

I said, "Well, I don't know if that's enough." But I agreed to be at the press conference the next day. I went to the Sheraton Hotel for the press conference. Terry McAuliffe, the Democratic Party chair, was there. Hillary Clinton was there. Chuck Schumer was there. All of the important Democratic political figures were there. As a party they apologized for what happened. And after the apology, I left. The press made a big deal about my leaving. Freddy endorsed Green, but I wasn't there to endorse Green, so I left.

Then the name of the person responsible for the race-baiting in Green's campaign came out and Green didn't fire him. So I refused to endorse him. The Friday night before the election, they had the Unity Dinner. Of course, I didn't go. There was a noticeable absence of blacks and Latinos. Bill and Hillary were there, and all the other usual suspects, but it was a lily white affair.

That night, Terry McAuliffe met with us. He asked, "How can we heal this?" I said "Mark Green was supposed to fire the person responsible for the race-baiting, and Green didn't do it. "

So Terry says, "Rev, I understand. All I'm asking is that you don't call for a boycott of the election."

"I'm not going to boycott the election," I told him. "But I'm not endorsing Mark Green."

At that point I had said that we might boycott the elections. But I couldn't boycott the election, because I wanted Bill Thompson to win as city controller. And there were a few people running for city council that we wanted to win.

On the Saturday before the elections, I do my morning radio broadcast where I urge folks to go out and vote. But I don't mention the mayor; I just tell them to vote for Bill Thompson and the folks for city council.

Monday I get a call from Ken Sunshine, a publicist who worked for Green and had done some work for me and for Jesse Jackson. He said, "Harvey Weinstein, who runs Miramax, wants to talk to you." I said, "All right."

He got Weinstein on the phone.

"Reverend Al. I hosted the dinner the other night and your absence was noticeable. We can't win this thing without the active support of both you and Freddy," he said.

"You may not notice, but the election is tomorrow," I said.

"Yeah, I know," he said. "But it's not too late. If y'all came out today and endorsed Mark Green it would make the six- and eleven-o'clock news and it will give us a guarantee."

I said, "All they had to do was fire these guys and show us some respect. I didn't start this. What you're asking me to do is to agree to race-baiting as a form of campaigning, and I'm not going to do that. I'm not going to sanction it. I'm not going to act like it's all right because it's not all right."

This is what Bill Clinton did to Jesse Jackson with Sister Souljah, and Jesse should have stopped it then. I was not going to do it. I would have rather gone through four more years of the crap we had been going through than for history to say that this guy used racial tactics and we let it go. I wasn't going to do that.

"My self-respect is not negotiable," I told him.

"Yes, but Bloomberg . . ."

I cut him off. "It ain't got nothing to do with Bloomberg. It has to do with my self-respect. I'm not endorsing Bloomberg.

"If someone violates me, you can't tell me, 'Well, someone else violated you more'—that still has nothing to do with the first person's violation of me."

"Can we talk about it?" he asked.

"Yeah."

We set up a meeting at the Four Seasons Hotel in the lobby in an hour. When I get there, I call Roberto and Freddy and they come. We talk and it finally comes down to this: If Mark Green promises that the guys responsible for the racial tactics will never be involved in a Green administration, then we will go with that.

It's now approaching five P.M.

I said, "How can I believe a guy who lied about even asking me for my support? You have to give me somebody who has something big to lose if he reneges. Someone we can believe."

"How about Bill Clinton?" Weinstein suggests.

"If you can get him to come over here and say that, we'll believe it," I said. "He's got something on the line—his wife."

Weinstein calls Bill Clinton. "Clinton will be here in twenty minutes," he said.

He rents a suite because the Secret Service doesn't want Clinton meeting in the lobby. We all go to the suite. Twenty minutes becomes an hour. An hour becomes two hours. Finally, hotel security says Bill Clinton is pulling up downstairs.

By now the press is everywhere. We were going to have a press conference after we met and endorsed Mark Green. Apparently, as Clinton is pulling up, Green's people call Clinton in the car and they tell him, "Don't do it. We don't want to cut a deal with them. We don't want to owe them."

Clinton pulls up and pulls off. They tell the press that the press spooked Clinton. How is the press going to spook Clinton? How were we going to have a press conference without the press?

Green's people didn't want it to appear to the white voters that he had actually played this race card and then had to cave in to me.

I went down to the press and announced that I was not going to endorse Green. "His people obviously don't want to deal with this," I said. New York 1 carried it live.

That night I get a call from Jonathan Capehart, an aid to Michael Bloomberg.

"So you didn't work out your arrangements with Mr. Green," he said.

I said, "No."

"I told everybody that there wouldn't be any deals with Mr. Sharpton," he said. "That it was a matter of self-respect."

"Well, Jonathan, we've come to know each other and you know I'm not going to do it. I'm just not going to bend," I said.

He says, "Hold on a minute."

And the voice on the other end said, "How are you doing?"

I said, "All right."

"If I win this you will always have access to City Hall," the voice said.

"Who is this?" I said.

"This is Mike Bloomberg."

Bloomberg had Jonathan call me to talk. We made no deals. We had met eight months before. But my stance had nothing to do with Bloomberg. It was all about Mark Green and this phony liberal stuff that he was trying to play on us.

The first time I talked to Bloomberg since I went to jail was that night.

The next day I come in and I'm fully prepared for Green's victory. I thought he would still win by a few points. I knew we had hurt him, but I never expected that he would lose. And I was prepared to battle with yet another mayor for four more years. That was all right, too, because I had just gone through eight years of war with Giuliani. And I went through twelve years with Ed Koch before that. So I was used to it.

Before the results are final, the press is all over talking about the turnout saying, "Al Sharpton is dead; blacks are going to vote for Green anyway." You would have thought I was running against Green.

That night, I went to the Bronx to Freddy and Roberto's headquarters. They have New York 1 on and Andrew Kirtzman, their political analyst, says, "It seems like a normal turnout. The Sharpton factor didn't work. Green is going to win. This might be a politically damaging time for Sharpton, who should have come in line."

On my cell phone, I get a call from Jonathan Capehart. He says, "Reverend Al, we're ahead."

I said, "Are you crazy? I'm looking at New York 1 and they have Green ahead by four points."

"We're getting our results straight from the Board of Elections," he said. "We're ahead."

"Are you serious?"

The polls close and Jonathan's on the phone telling me they have won. But New York 1 has Green ahead and they're still saying that our nonendorsement of Green had no impact. All night long it's back and forth. Finally around eleven o'clock, the news starts turning around. Then Mark Green is forced to concede.

You would have thought we'd won the election. The people in the Bronx were going crazy, jumping up and down.

Then, all of a sudden it went from me being the no-factor guy to "Al Sharpton defeats Mark Green." "It's Al Sharpton's fault." The same reporters who were saying that I was dead were giving me all the credit for Green's defeat.

To this day, I feel that the Democratic Party had to be taught a lesson and still has to be taught one nationally. We did not get the right to vote from the Democrats or the Republicans. Our grandparents went out there and faced dog bites, jail cells, and some died. And before I take that vote and give it to somebody who doesn't respect me, I would rather sit up until hell freezes over.

My mother used to tell me while she was battling my father for child support that rather than suffer the indignity, she would sit up in court every day, wrap a peanut butter and jelly sandwich, until she got justice. "Because your dignity should never be compromised," she would say.

A lot of 2004 will be about what happened in New York in 2001. It's about dignity. Blacks and Latinos and progressives have voted in unusual numbers for Democrats. Ninety-five percent of the black vote went for Gore in 2000. And we don't have a black in the United States Senate? We don't have a black governor. The Democrats won't take a strong stand on Affirmative Action. They won't deal with the disproportionate number of blacks and Latinos in jail. Welfare reform put people in these work programs, and now these people are back on the streets. How can we continue not to challenge the party that got 95 percent of our vote? We can't as long as they can take us for granted.

The Democratic Party acts like we are their mistress that they have to hide, like we're some political scarlet whore rather than their respected partner. Either we're going to have a healthy marriage or we're getting a divorce and marrying someone who will respect us. We will no longer allow ourselves to be screwed by the Democrats.

I didn't call for a boycott. I voted on Election Day. And cast my vote for Thompson and others. But my arm just couldn't reach for the lever next to Mark Green. I just couldn't do it. There was power in not casting that vote.

And it is that power that blacks, Latinos, and anyone who is disenfranchised by the system must exert.

This is the message to the Democratic Party in 2004: Don't take us for granted.

CHAPTER SIXTEEN

★

LEADERSHIP: BLACK POWER

The day Dr. Martin Luther King Jr. was shot is still so vivid in my memory. It was like yesterday. I was in the living room of our tiny two-bedroom apartment in the projects in Brooklyn. I was watching *Ironside,* with Raymond Burr. My mother and I watched that show every week. In the middle of the show, a news flash cut in across the screen with the words "Martin Luther King Jr. has been shot in Memphis."

My mother began to cry. She cried like it was her own brother who had been shot. About an hour later, they broke in again to say that Martin Luther King was dead. I was sad. I worked in his Breadbasket program and was a youth minister. I met Dr. King a couple of times. He knew me as "the boy preacher." When he would see me, he would say,

"There goes that boy preacher!" and a big grin would break over his face. I felt good being a part of something he was involved in, and the loss was definitely felt. But my mother's reaction—how hard she took it—confused me.

I asked her about it. And she told me why she took his death so personally. My mother was raised in Alabama, in the heart of the Deep South. She said to me, "If you grew up having to sit at the back of the bus, if you were ever thirsty and saw only a 'Whites only' water fountain and could not get a drink, if you were hungry and couldn't go to a restaurant and be served, then you would know why I'm crying so hard."

I understood her intellectually, but I didn't feel what she was saying until about a year later. I went to see a movie at the Loews Theater on Flatbush Avenue in Brooklyn. They were showing *King: From Montgomery to Memphis*, a documentary on his thirteen-year career. At the end of the movie, Nina Simone sang this song: "Why? The King of Love is Dead." She sang, "Turn down your TV set; love your neighbor was his plea," and she asked, "What we gonna do now that the king of love is dead?" That's when it hit me. All those things he did, all those freedoms he fought for, all those laws that got overturned to make life better for all people—what would happen now?

What we gonna do? We couldn't just act like, now that King was gone, everything he worked for would stop. As Nina Simone sang her song, they showed Dr. King's funeral procession. There were horses carrying his body, a horse-drawn wagon with his casket in a glass case trotting through town. That image was all I could think about for days.

I sat there and made up my mind that there was something I had to do. I had to try and keep his legacy alive. I was only fourteen years old, but I knew I could do something, that I must do something. I went back to Breadbasket and asked if I could be youth director and began my journey to carry on Dr. King's legacy.

Time has been one of the greatest teachers in allowing me to make my own mistakes and grow and learn. Dr. King was the first major teacher in leadership 101 that I had.

I also learned about leadership from Nelson Mandela. He sustained his position and never gave up the fight. Somewhere inside, he had the strength to endure torture and more than two and a half decades of imprisonment because he believed he was right. He could see it. And after thirty years of fighting, apartheid was lifted and one man, one vote was instituted. Only a real leader could make that happen.

I met Nelson Mandela in 1993, on his second trip to the United States. He came to address the United Nations and ask them to stop sanctions against South Africa. Our sanctions were left over from our protests over apartheid. And with that government displaced and South Africa moving toward a democratic election (which eventually led to Mandela's being president there), Mandela felt it was okay for America to start doing business with South Africa again.

Before he addressed the UN, a group of about twenty black leaders met with him.

The next time I saw Mandela was in South Africa, to observe their very first democratic election. There was an air and aura of greatness around him. He was secure and so committed that he embodied the principles that he represented.

With great leaders there is no gap between who they are and their mission. That's the only thing that would make someone spend twenty-seven years in jail and never waver in his mission or belief. And it is the enduring of those hard times that strengthens a leader.

I arrived at that place in my soul while on a gurney at Coney Island Hospital with a knife wound in my chest. I came to the realization that I was willing to die for justice. I realized I was willing to take it all for the cause. That resolve strengthened over the ninety days I spent in jail fighting for the rights of others to live free from government intrusion and harm. Those are the times when you find yourself. When you look back and you know that you would take every one of those experiences again, you close the gap between your mission and yourself. And the more effective you are as a leader.

Adam Clayton Powell Jr. was instrumental in shaping my role as a leader. He was responsible for a lot of the attitudes I have today about being a leader.

I met him when I was about eleven years old. I convinced my mother to let me go to Abyssinian Baptist Church to see him preach.

As a kid I would read to escape. I didn't want to play with the other kids because they would tease me, so I found this new world in books. I found this one book, by a guy named Claude Lewis, about Powell, and I became totally mesmerized. I used to watch Powell on the news and clip articles about him in the newspaper. I finally convinced my mother to let me go see him.

In those days black mothers in Brooklyn used to say that Harlem was dangerous. I couldn't just go to Harlem. And Harlem mothers used to say Brooklyn was dangerous. But after much nagging, she finally let me go. But I had to go with my sister.

We rode the train to Harlem and I was so excited. It was crowded, but we found a seat near the front. The choir was singing and when the minister came out, it wasn't Powell. He was away. I was so disappointed. And I had to wait something like three months before my mother would let me go again.

The second time I went to Abyssinian, he was there. I'll never forget to this day the first time I actually laid eyes on Adam Clayton Powell Jr. He walked out of the side door into the sanctuary in his robe, with that straight, strong posture. He walked up those marble stairs to the semicircular pulpit. I thought I had seen God.

I don't believe I have ever been as impressed seeing a

human being as I was seeing Adam Clayton Powell Jr. that day. He had this magnetism and this majestic air. He was very elegant, but at the same time defiant—a real man's man. Self-assured, confident.

At the end of the service, I made my way back to the pastor's office. I had been preaching myself since I was four years old, and I knew the ins and outs of church—where the minister went after the service and what he did.

I walked up to the pastor's office, with my sister right behind me, and I knocked. In those days they had doors that were split in half, and the secretary opened the top half and looked out. She could barely see me over the door. Finally, she looked down and said, "May I help you, son?" I said, "Yes, I would like to see Reverend Powell."

"You would like to do what?!"

I said, "I'd like to see Reverend Powell."

She started laughing and said, "Who may I tell Reverend Powell is calling?"

"Reverend Al Sharpton."

She laughed again, turned and went on about her business. After I realized she didn't take me seriously, I knocked again. She came back, this time a little annoyed, and I told her again that I wanted to see Reverend Powell. She went somewhere and came back with a real puzzled look on her face and said, "Follow me."

I followed her and she brought me to this room, and Adam Clayton Powell Jr. was standing there with no shirt on, no undershirt, just his pants. He had changed out of his sweaty clothes from his sermon. He was standing there with his arms around one of the older matrons of the church, just talking to her. And he turned around and looked at me and said, "Alfred Sharpton! Boy preacher from Brooklyn."

I looked at him and said, "You know me?"

"Of course I do," he said. "I listen to F. D. Washington's radio program in New York."

Rev. Washington was my bishop and he featured me on his radio broadcasts.

"Sit down, son," he said.

By now I'm in seventh heaven—Adam Clayton Powell, my hero, actually knew me. My sister and I sat down while he got dressed. And he invited us to go to the Red Rooster, a local bar/restaurant, to have a drink with him.

"I can't drink," I said. "I'm only eleven years old!"

"You can have a Coca-Cola, can't you?" he said.

And that began a regular routine for us. When he was in town, I would meet up with him in Harlem and we'd just go hang out. I'd go get the coffee, run errands, do whatever I could. I used to love to just see him sitting in the back of the Red Rooster, holding court with some of the biggest, most prominent people you would see in the news. They would all come up and go see Adam Powell. And they started saying people came to kiss the ring of Adam Clayton Powell. Growing up, seeing this black preacher wielding this kind of awesome power, with defiance, inspired me. What I learned from Powell about leadership—and Adam Powell is probably the only man I ever met like this—is that you can't care what people think. Adam Clayton Powell did not care about being accepted by society.

The only other man in my life who was like this was James Brown, but Adam Clayton Powell taught me this valuable lesson first. You cannot be a true leader if you care about what people think or say about you. Powell was on the David Frost Show once. Frost hosted one of the more popular syndicated talk shows back in the 1960s. The show was taped at the Little Theatre on Forty-fourth Street in the middle of the theater district. David Frost asked Powell, "Reverend Powell, you have been a member of Congress for over twenty years, and you pastor one of the largest congregations in the world, yet you have been married four times; you drink liquor publicly; you have girlfriends; you have been indicted for tax evasion and sued. How do you rationalize all this?"

Powell looked at him and with a smirk said, "Don't be jealous, baby. Don't be jealous." Frost followed that question up with, "How would Adam Clayton Powell describe Adam Clayton Powell?" Powell looked at him and said, "I'm probably the only man in America—black or white—who doesn't give a damn."

"A damn about what?" Frost asked.

"A damn about what you all think of me or write about me," Powell said. "If it's not illegal, immoral, or fattening, Adam Clayton Powell is going to do what he believes is right."

Adam Clayton Powell Jr. had power. He had the inside track. He could get where he wanted, but he never lost that defiance. He always did it his way. And while some people said it was his downfall, I always admired that about him. I don't justify any of the things Powell did. And I don't judge him, either. I know a lot of preachers who are immoral. Powell did what he did in the open. We used to drive around town in an old station wagon owned by his bodyguard, Jack Packett. I used to crawl into the back and ride with them when I could. One day when we were riding, Powell turns to me and said, "Kid?" (He used to call me kid.)

"Yes, sir?"

He said, "Don't ever forget this: If you expose your own weaknesses, they can never use them against you. 'Cause can't nobody tell what everybody already knows. What might appear to be reckless behavior on my part is really defense. They can never threaten to expose me, because I expose myself." And that's true. I loved Adam Clayton Powell for his defiance and his sense of who he was. I, probably more than anybody in public life, talk about Adam Clayton Powell. I always felt that I owed it to him to keep his legacy alive. One of my dreams is to stand up in front of the Democratic National Convention and talk about him, because nobody did more for social legislation in America than Adam Clayton Powell. Nobody made sure my mother wasn't marginalized. Twenty years before the Montgomery bus boycott, Powell led the Harlem boycott. He taught civil disobedience to King's generation, and he got more laws passed than anybody who has ever been in Congress—before or after him. And for him to only be remembered as a playboy and all that, is ridiculous.

He died on April 4, 1972. A couple of days later, the *New York Times* ran an editorial that I will never erase from my memory. It said something to the effect that on April 4, black America lost two giants: one in 1968, in Dr. Martin Luther King Jr.; and one in 1972, in Adam Clayton Powell Jr. One left a legacy; the other did not. One was great; the other wasn't. It went on to continue to ridicule Powell and all that he had accomplished, and to extol King. And I thought it was an absolute insult. For the *Times* to vilify someone who I believed to be one of our heroes and to make the silly comparisons as if black America must choose, I thought was irresponsible. And certainly, as a confirmed, die-hard Adamite, it was something I will always resent.

Adam Clayton Powell Jr. was one of America's greatest leaders and should be remembered first and foremost as such. America cannot tell me who my leaders are or should be.

There was a cover of *Newsweek* in January 2002 that featured American Express CEO Ken Chenault, Merrill Lynch President Stan O'Neal, and Dick Parsons, CEO of AOL Time Warner, with the headline "The New Black Power." What black power do they represent? If their predominantly white board of directors decided tomorrow to replace anyone of them, Chenault, O'Neal, and Parsons would be unemployed. None of them are accountable to black people; they were not chosen by black people. It is an insult to say to the black community that they are the new black power. If I said that the new white leadership in this country is Gerald Levin, who Dick Parsons replaced, white folks would say I was crazy. If I said George Bush doesn't represent white America, Tom Daschle doesn't represent white America, Donald Trump does—that's ridiculous.

Are they now suggesting that if someone shoots Mrs. Diallo's son, they should call Dick Parsons? Are they now suggesting that if there is another Abner Louima case, they should go see Ken Chenault? Of course, we have black businessmen now in powerful positions, and we're proud of them. And they are qualified and capable. But they have, for the most part, gotten where they have as a result of the work that Dr. King and others marched and were killed for. They are there because we fought to get the corporate world open. Because of those efforts, we now have black CEOs.

Rather than say they're "the new black power"—to suggest that they are an alternative to civil rights leaders—understand that they need the "real black power" just as much as the rest of us. In this whole obsession of America to control the definitions of leadership for black folks, they make the results the responses. If you want to know about the new black power, why not feature the blacks who started their own businesses, who own their own businesses? Ken Chenault doesn't own American Express. Dick Parsons doesn't own AOL Time Warner. Their power isn't even economic black power. These are blacks in powerful positions, but they do not represent black power.

There's a difference between black leaders and leading blacks. What white media has tried to do is to say that leading blacks are black leaders. There's not one black I know who will say they're following Dick Parsons or Ken Chenault—including them. The fact is, when some of them get in trouble, they call me. Earl Graves Jr., the son of the founder of *Black Enterprise* magazine, was racially profiled in a train station on his way into New York City. He called us. Graves is the chair of the Madison Avenue Initiative of National Action Network. It was created for those wealthy businessmen who own magazines and radio stations but cannot get the same ad dollar as their white counterparts. They cannot call Stan O'Neal for help. They still face racism—even at their level. And they need black leaders and activists to fight for them.

But it goes back to white America defining for black people who our leaders should be. The images that are projected are subtle. To justify black progress, using one or two successful blacks as an example, is racist. And it doesn't begin to deal with the entire differences between the life of the average person of color in America and an average white in America. I often hear people who question how I became a leader and I tell them, "If there were no injustice, if there were no racism, there would be no need for an Al Sharpton."

CHAPTER SEVENTEEN

★

JESSE JACKSON

I met the Reverend Jesse Jackson for the first time when I was about twelve years old. I was still very much the boy preacher in Brooklyn. I had just started edging toward joining the Civil Rights Movement. I had been mesmerized by Adam Clayton Powell, one of the first blacks in Congress, the pastor at Abyssinian Baptist Church and an activist. When I met Jesse he reminded me of Powell—very charismatic and flamboyant.

This was the late 1960's; Dr. Martin Luther King Jr. had just been killed, and everybody was becoming far more militant. People were moving away from the nonviolent protesting of Dr. King. My pastor at the Temple Church of God in Christ, Bishop F. D. (which stood for Frederick Douglass) Washington, saw what was happening and didn't want to see me heading in that direction—joining the Black Panthers or some other "revolutionary" group.

Bishop Washington brought me to Operation Bread-basket, part of the King movement. It was headed in Brooklyn by the Reverend William Jones (who is my pastor today). Jesse came to Breadbasket one day, and that's when we met. He was in his late twenties, and right away we identified with each other. Jesse was younger than the other preachers of that time. He wouldn't even wear a suit and tie. Jesse always used to wear a medallion like Adam. And he sported the buck vest and a big 'fro.

I later learned that he had been born out of wedlock and came from a broken home, like I did. He didn't come out of the seminary, wasn't one of those collegiate types. He wasn't like that. Jesse was regular. They used to call him "Reverend Jesse," and he used to call himself, "the Country Preacher."

We just hit it off. I became his protégé. I started wearing medallions like his and I used to try to talk like him. He would call me a lot on the phone and we would meet when he was in town. I got to know Mrs. Jackson very well, and during that time we became very close.

So down through the years we were always close. My mother loved him. He was part of the family. Even when we would argue, it was like arguing with a family member—it never lasted long. We would never really grow but so distant. The only problem Jesse and I had early on was my relationship with James Brown. Jesse thought that my relationship with James would be a distraction to my civil rights work.

Jesse may have been a little jealous because I was so close to James Brown, who had become a father figure—a role Jesse had held. I didn't pay Jesse any mind, though. I used to tell him, "You're close to Hollywood; why can't I be close to James Brown?" Jesse was real close with Berry Gordy, Sammy Davis Jr., and Quincy Jones, but he had a problem with me hanging out with James Brown? He soon got over it.

But in the late 1980s, there was a rift over my closeness to the nationalist crowd. Jesse would say, "What are you doing? That's not what you come out of!"

Jesse used to catch a lot of flak from the nationalists because he carried on Dr. King's vision of integration. And they would call him a sellout and a tool of the party—even then.

In 1972, the National Black Political Convention in Gary, Indiana was the first place where I actually saw the tension between Jesse and the nationalists. I was eighteen years old, the youngest guy on the platform. They introduced Jesse to speak, and Jesse was very popular nationwide. But he got booed soundly at the convention. He was able to quiet the crowd and quell the boos. Jesse ended up delivering one of the best speeches he had ever given, and by the end of it those same guys who had been booing were cheering him. But the tension between Jesse and the nationalists continued.

When Jesse ran for president in 1984, there was tension. But Minister Louis Farrakhan, of the Nation of Islam, was the one who kept the nationalists from attacking Jesse during his run for president.

But I was always tight with the nationalists, and that created some distance between Jesse and me. We would talk off and on, but it was clear to me that we weren't as tight as we used to be. And we continued to drift apart until I got stabbed in 1991.

I was in surgery for a while after the stabbing.

When they finally brought me into the recovery room, I was lying there and looked up and saw David Dinkins. I had known Dinkins since I was a kid. He was my attorney who incorporated my National Youth Movement when I was still "the boy preacher." I used to visit him frequently when he was the city clerk of New York. I used to go down to his office in the Municipal Building and just hang out. He took me to lunch one of the first times I met him at his office. There was a vegetarian store near the Municipal Building, and he took me there. He said, "I want to introduce you to some health food." "Health food?" "Yes, health food," he said. So we went and had this salad. After lunch, I got back on the train and eventually went home. My mother asked, "How was your lunch with Mr. Dinkins?" I said, "He's a weird guy. He likes to eat grass and lettuce!" That was my first memory of David Dinkins.

But around the time of the Brawley case, we had gotten distant. He never told me directly that he disapproved of the way I handled the case; he just became distant. Then, in 1992, when I ran for the Senate, he supported Bob Abrams against me.

But he put our difference aside for a minute after I was stabbed in 1991. After surgery, they took me to recovery. I was really groggy, but I looked up and there were four guys standing around my bed with masks on. They took off the surgical masks and there was Dave Dinkins, Deputy Mayor Bill Lynch, Deputy Mayor Milton Mollen, and Police Commissioner Lee Brown, who went on to become Mayor of Houston, Texas.

"Oh, no!" I said. "I died and went to hell!" And we all had a good laugh.

After Dinkins and the others left, they let Kathy in. She was going to spend the night in recovery, and they were getting her a cot.

A nurse brought me a note that said, "Your father called." I had not heard from my father since I was a kid, but I knew he had moved somewhere in Florida. And the number on the note was a Florida number.

I thought, "I've been indicted, been to jail, now he's calling?! What am I going to call him for?"

Kathy took the note and she didn't say anything. I asked her to find me a cell phone. She got a cell phone, thinking I was probably going to call my father. But I called Jesse. He was in Washington at the time, and when he picked up I said, "Reverend, I don't know if you've heard, but I got stabbed today."

He said, "Are you all right?"

"I think I'll be all right," I said.

"Al, I keep telling you it's dangerous out there. You have to take your work seriously."

While we were on the phone, the news of my stabbing flashed across the television. I could hear Jackie crying in the background. And I could tell that Jesse was crying, too. He told me he was coming east that week and that he would see me in a few days.

"We haven't talked in a long time," he said. "It's time for us to sit down and talk."

The doctors came in later and said I shouldn't make any calls. That call to Jesse was the only call I made, except for one to my mother.

At 8:30 the next morning they said they were going to move me out of recovery and into a private room. Kathy spent the night with me in recovery, and at about seven A.M., they came and woke me up and wheeled me into the private room, and Jesse was there.

He said, "Boy, Jackie was so upset about you I had to cancel my schedule and come see you."

He hugged me and we talked for a long while. Over the next few days we began reconciling. It was in that hospital that I decided I would start National Action Network and that I was going to go back more toward civil rights work on a permanent level and run for office. I ended up running for the Senate in New York the next year.

When I got out of the hospital, our families conspired to

get us together again. Jackie Jackson's birthday was in March, so we all decided I was going to Vegas for recovery and we would have a surprise birthday party for her. Jesse and I spent maybe four or five days together planning this party and really bonding again.

Over the next six or seven years we talked every day—sometimes two and three times a day. Every time he came to New York, I would ride around with him—no matter what I was doing, I dropped it so that I could be with him. I learned a lot being around him. Jesse Jackson is probably the smartest person I know. There's no one I know who has a more brilliant, fertile mind. He is hardworking. I learned about the value of getting up early every morning from Jesse. And he is very, very committed.

But I began to question the direction that commitment was taking in the late 1990s. Jesse had developed a closeness to Bill Clinton. And I felt his relationship with Clinton and the White House was getting in the way of his work as an activist. I felt that if he was going to represent the civil rights cause, the human rights cause, Jesse had to choose between whether he was going to be part of the structure or challenge the structure. Dr. King, as close as he was to Lyndon Johnson, came out vocally against the war in Vietnam. He never took a presidential appointment. He challenged the system.

There's nothing wrong with working from within the system. There is a legitimate role for that. You had Whitney Young and others who were close to the system. But you can't be Dr. King and Whitney Young at the same time. You need both, but you can't be both. And where I started having levels of tactical discomfort with Jesse was over this issue. You can't be the insider on Wall Street and challenge Wall Street. You can't advise the president and be the insider to the White House, and challenge the president. While Jesse was inside the White House with Clinton, I was outside calling for economic accountability on Wall Street. I was outside, calling Clinton's hand on welfare reform and the onerous crime bill. Jesse was virtually silent on those issues. He was an insider. And after seven years of us being close again, we started to split.

Contrary to popular belief, we didn't split over his scandal with Karen Stafford and the baby he had out of wedlock. We divided over philosophy.

Our split became public when a young man named LeVan Hawkins came to me looking for help. He was promised 225 Burger King franchises. He built half of them and it got backed up, and there was some litigation that ended with Burger King pulling the deal. Mr. Hawkins asked me to go to Burger King on his behalf.

Burger King said Mr. Hawkins had done some things that they didn't agree with. And I said, "But you made a commitment to the black community to build these stores. Even if you don't do it with Mr. Hawkins, you can fulfill your commitment with somebody else."

They said no. And I led a boycott of Burger King in New

York. Jesse publicly disagreed with the boycott, and that's when we started having public disagreements.

I couldn't believe that he, who taught me in my youth about fighting these corporations and making them accountable, would publicly come out against my doing the very thing he'd taught me how to do.

It was very painful. I felt that if anyone understood what I was doing (including my run for president), it would be Jesse because he had been through much of what I was going through. To see Jesse on the other side publicly was painful. And though he never criticized me personally (although many reporters have told me that he has done so privately), that he would take a different position was personal enough repudiation. It was something, however, that I had to bear.

My only comfort was history. I remembered that Jesse had to deal with many around Dr. King, like Andy Young and Mrs. King, who wouldn't support him when he ran for president. They wouldn't support him in some boycotts. I thought, "Maybe I'm going through the same thing with him that he went through with others." But I would have thought that he might not want to do that to the next generation.

I am grateful for my recent experience with Jesse. It has forced me to grow in many areas and take stock of where I am and where I'm going. It has helped me to better define for myself what it takes to be an effective leader, and it has helped me avoid some of the mistakes I've seen around me. I have learned that one of the first things you have to decide in leadership is that you cannot be all things to all people. You have to make up your mind what tradition of leadership you're going to be in, and stick with the program. There are many schools of thought and many traditions of leadership.

When I spoke at the Million Man March, I said, "We all come from different houses but we're all on the same block." There's the NAACP house, those who fight on the inside along with the system. There's the legal house, the Thurgood Marshalls, the lawyers who use constitutional law to fight. There's the Urban League, which deals with the corporate inside. There are those who fight from the outside using nonviolent protest—the civil rights house. There are the elected officials—Adam Clayton Powell and Harold Washington—representing that house. But you cannot live in all houses—you start looking like a vagabond, a nomad, or a homeless person. There are ups and downs with any house. There are the assets and liabilities. But you must choose—this is my comfort zone, this is my calling, and I'm going to take the flak and the praise, whatever comes. And that's your house. That's where you live. Jesse wouldn't stay in his house.

I would sit with guys my age, guys like Greg Meeks, who is now in Congress, and David Patterson, who is in the state senate of New York, and we would all discuss our roles and where we were. My role has always been to help set a climate. Their job was to go inside the system. Mine was to help set a climate so they could operate inside that system. My job has been to try to create a climate around issues like police brutality so they could create police brutality legislation. But if they did what I did, they couldn't get inside to make laws. They couldn't get elected. They couldn't get Republicans or moderate Democrats to vote for their bills.

But if they didn't have somebody like me helping to set the climate, they wouldn't even have an issue from which to deal. My criticism of guys like Jesse is that you can't be in and out. If you decide to go in, stay in and let those who are still out do our jobs. But don't go in and run out, go in and run out.

Not to say you can't help change the system using the system. I ran for the Senate. My running helped change the climate. I ran for mayor. My running helped change the climate. I'm running for president, my running will change the climate.

I run for office as an outsider. If I win, I then become an insider and have to give up my work as an activist. If I had won my run for the Senate or mayor of New York, I would not be up every Saturday trying to lead a movement. I would have acquiesced that to someone else. I would have supported them and met with them. But I would not be in and out at the same time.

If I win this next race—and I am running to win—I will be president. That's what I'll be. I will give up my other job.

I'm not going to try to be the president and the protestor of the president. If I don't win (and I'm certainly not running to lose), and if I decide to advise the president, whoever the president is, then I'm not going to lead the Movement.

I cannot tell the Movement, "Now wait a minute, I'm wearing this hat at eleven, but at twelve, I'm the leader of the Movement." Either you are or you are not.

I'm running for president as one who is in the forefront of a movement of issues that have not been addressed. So I'm in my role.

Jesse ran as an outsider. But when he became an insider, that's what he needed to focus on. And he earned the right to be an insider; I take nothing away from him for that. But say that's what you're doing. The Bible says, "No man can serve two masters."

And I understand maturation and change. At different stages in life you do different things. David, the warrior who slew Goliath, was not the same man as King David. You have a right to be king. But if you're king, you cannot also be the warrior fighting against the powers that be. And as king, you must also respect those who are still the warriors. But you don't try to do both. When you do, you not only confuse the masses, you also confuse your own spirit because you're not focused, you're not disciplined, you're not moving forward. And you're not an effective leader.

CHAPTER EIGHTEEN

★

I'M BLACK AND I'M PROUD

I know I am an enigma to many people. Folks can't understand why, in the twenty-first century, I still wear my hair
this way. They don't understand why I talk the way I do.
Why I walk the way I do. Andrew Cooper, publisher of the
City Sun, a weekly black newspaper, explained in 1988 why
many whites found me so easy to hold in contempt. "He's
fat; he has show-business hair, a gold medal, a jumpsuit,
and Reeboks. He's a perfect stereotype of a pork chop preacher." But I never embraced that stereotype.

When I was four years old I decided what I was going to
be. I knew I was going to be a preacher. I used to come home
from church on Sundays, line up my sister's dolls, and
preach the sermon I had heard earlier in church. I did this
just about every day. And when my mother saw this, she

brought me to my pastor, who encouraged me to do it. Had my mother stopped me or had my pastor said, "You're too little to preach; you can't do that," I may not be where I am today. Having people in my life who encouraged my whims and goals instead of squashing them before they were able to blossom had a significant impact on my life.

I have often said that I have been extremely blessed to be surrounded by greatness. Growing up, I met Dr. Martin Luther King Jr. He inspired me to be a civil rights activist, and it is his methods that I use today to fight injustices. I was raised in the movement by Jesse Jackson, one of the smartest men I have ever known. I was greatly influenced by Adam Clayton Powell Jr., whose uncompromising will and courage helped change the way we live today. I took things from him and his style of activism. But the person who had the greatest influence over me and is most responsible for the man I am today is James Brown. He had more impact on my life than any civil rights leader—maybe even more than my own mother. What I learned from him makes it possible for me to do the things I do today.

The first time I set eyes on James Brown was when I was a little boy. My father was a fan of his. He used to wear his hair like James Brown, which made me want to do the same thing. Whenever James Brown performed in New York at the Apollo Theater, my father found a way for us to get tickets. And we always got seats right up front. It was one of the few good memories I have of being with my father. Little did I know that years later I would actually get to know

James Brown personally. Teddy, James Brown's son, was a member of my National Youth Movement. We were really close. Teddy was his favorite son, and when he was killed at age seventeen in a car accident, James Brown sort of adopted me.

When I turned seventeen and graduated from high school, he asked my mother if I could travel with him and sort of be his road manager. James Brown used to travel with a bag of cash. He would have $30,000 to $40,000—and as much as $100,000—in cash in this green bag at any given time. And I was one of the few people on this earth whom he trusted. "I know Rev won't steal from me," he would say. So my job was to carry his bag around the country. But my real job was just to be his son. James Brown taught me about being a man. He gave me life skills that I never got from my own father. He taught me about self-respect, dignity, and self-definition.

James Brown grew up in Augusta, Georgia, in the segregated, Jim Crow South. He endured being called everything but a child of God. No black person at that time was called by their surname or with the respectful title of Mr. or Mrs. They were either "boy" or "girl" or "George" or "Sally." So when James Brown formed his band, he demanded that everybody be called Mr. or Mrs. with their surname. When I met my wife, Kathy, who sang in James Brown's band, she was Miss Jordan. James Brown has never called me Al. He has always called me Reverend. That's the way it was. No compromise. No exceptions. James Brown was booked to do *The Tonight Show,* starring Johnny Carson, which was the hottest show of that time. We were all very excited and we packed up to go to Hollywood. James Brown would perform on television in front of 40 million viewers. He had arrived. While the band and everybody was backstage getting ready to do their thing, Johnny Carson came into the dressing room to meet James Brown.

"Hey, James!" Johnny Carson said with a broad smile.

"You know, Mr. Carson, I have a thing about people calling me by my first name. You call me Mr. Brown and I'll call you Mr. Carson," James Brown said.

"Oh, Jimmy, we don't do that around here," Carson said, slapping James Brown on the back. "You'll always be Jimmy around here."

James Brown looked at me and said, "Rev, tell the band to pack up." And he made us leave right then and there. We did not do *The Tonight Show.* All the way back to the hotel I kept thinking, "Man, this was Johnny Carson! He would have been seen by forty million people." And I asked James Brown about it.

He said, "Reverend, it's not to *be* seen; it's *how* you're seen.

"If I'm not going to be seen tonight by forty million people, then at least I can look at myself in the mirror. I'm not going to let anyone disrespect me. I built myself from a shoeshine boy to a superstar. But I didn't do that to be nobody's boy. I did that to be a man."

He wouldn't do Ronald Reagan's inauguration because

he felt they disrespected him. It's an honor to perform at the president's inauguration. But James said, "There is no honor in being disrespected."

That's one of the best lessons I learned from James Brown—never compromise your dignity for any amount of success, any amount of fame, any amount of money. Your dignity and self-respect is more valuable than any of those things. I also learned the importance of self-definition. When the world looked at James Brown and was calling him a monkey, he looked in the mirror and saw a superstar. When the world was calling him "nigga," he saw a strong black man. He could write, "Say it loud; I'm black and I'm proud!" after growing up in a place where blacks were forced to sit at the backs of buses, and where they hung signs "For Coloreds" to drink out of separate water fountains. Here was a man with an enormous vision for himself.

James Brown rose to fame in an era when black people were, by and large, disrespected and treated as "less than." Even among black people, James Brown wasn't accepted. He was short; he was very dark, bowlegged; he didn't have a single Caucasian feature. Many considered him ugly. But he made it; he became successful because he worked hard and he never let anyone define for him who he was.

"Reverend, you know in the late nineteen-sixties when I started there were all those pretty, yellow boys," he would say. "There was Smokey Robinson, Jackie Wilson, Sam Cooke. I had to beat them all. I had to figure out how to get past all of them."

One night he was playing a club in Baltimore and got a call from his booking agent, Jack Bach, with Universal Attractions.

"Mr. Brown, I got a problem and I need you to help me out," Jack Bach said.

"What's that, Mr. Bach," James Brown said.

"Jackie [Wilson]'s drunk again and he is supposed to play the Howard Theatre," Mr. Bach said. "He's drunk at some hotel and can't perform. Maybe most people will walk out on you, but maybe some won't and we save some of our money." The Howard Theatre in Washington, D.C., was *the* spot back then. And to perform there meant you had arrived. So James Brown and the Flames jumped in a couple of cars and drove an hour and half to D.C. When they got there, they made the announcement that Jackie Wilson would not be performing. People started getting up and walking out, James Brown told me. But the Flames started playing anyway, and James Brown came on stage and started dancing.

"I just knew in my heart, this was it, this was my big shot—and I took it," James Brown said. "People turned around and started looking and I saw a cord that was hanging off the side of the stage. And I found myself, Rev, climbing up the side of the stage and grabbing the cord. I swung onto the stage and came down in a perfect split and then popped up. By then the whole audience turned around and sat down. I danced until my joints were sore. The next night, they announced that Jackie Wilson was back and people said, 'No, we want to see that little guy who looks like a monkey, dance.'" "That's when I took Washington," James Brown said. "From there I started beating Jackie all over the country."

They had the same booking agents, and it was pure determination that gave James Brown the edge. They called James Brown the hardest-working man in show business, and it was true.

It was that kind of determination that he instilled in me. He would say, "You're a James Brown kind of guy. You came out of the hard-core ghetto. You ain't like some of these other guys." And that's how I grew up. James Brown also taught me about not compromising what I believe. Even when I was touring with James Brown, I always went to church. That's how Kathy and I became close—because she was one of the only members of James Brown's band who went to church every Sunday. I don't care where we were on the road; she would get up on Sunday and go to somebody's church. Finally, we got James Brown going to church, too.

I was never ashamed of "Amazing Grace," never cared who didn't like my hair, and never ever felt that I had to prove anything to white people. James Brown taught me to be myself. After James Brown had gone through a rough period in his career, John Belushi and Dan Akroyd reached out to him for a movie they were doing called *The Blues Brothers*. They wanted him to play a preacher in their movie. James Brown took it, and I even helped him rehearse for the part.

On the set, they had this whole church scene set up. They had a choir in the background singing, "Let's All Go Back to the Old Landmark," and James Brown was to come out in his preacher's robe and deliver his sermon. He came out and did his famous James Brown slide out to the pulpit. He did his spin and his split and was dancing during the song. The director stopped him and said, "Wait a minute, Mr. Brown, you have to calm down."

James Brown looked at him and said, "If you wanted Frank Sinatra, you should have booked him. If you want James Brown, this is what you get."

Those were defining moments for me. James Brown taught me never to let people define who you are. I asked him later why he stood his ground with those Hollywood people. He said, "If you start letting people define who you are, people will then decide what is credible and what is not. And you never give them that, Rev. You may suffer, but you never give them that."

James Brown even taught me how to overcome adversity. He got into trouble with the law later in his career, and I went to see him in jail. I went when some of his kids wouldn't go see him. I thought I would see him broken and down. But when I walked into that cell, the first thing he said to me was, "Rev, when I get out of here, they're going to have the biggest show in the world. We're going to have to plan the return of James Brown." And I'm thinking, "That's crazy. His career is over." But he was right. I lived to see it. Two years later, he went to Hollywood and everybody who was anybody was there for the return of James Brown. He sat in his dressing room that night getting ready to perform. I was the only one he let in the dressing room.

He rarely socialized in the dressing room throughout his career. He would say, "I'm not here to meet and greet, I'm not here for no games. I'm here to work." He said, "Reverend, the problem with most blacks is that they're into show. And whites are in show business. I'm not into show. I'm in show *business*. This is not about taking pictures or running with girls; this is about business." Even when I was on the road with him, he would always tell me, "I better not catch you drinking or hanging with loose women!"

Now, he would go out after a show and have a drink, but he was very strict on me. Because he promised my mother that he would look after me. I was seventeen or eighteen in Hollywood and Las Vegas, had never seen that kind of lifestyle, but he was hard on me.

Now I understand why God had me be around a man like James Brown. I would not have learned those lessons hanging with some of the guys in the Civil Rights Movement. They didn't have that kind of fortitude and that kind of integrity and internal strength. They didn't have that kind of self-respect and self-definition. They didn't have to overcome the kinds of things James Brown overcame to be a success. I had to see that. I had to know how to be an underdog and come out a winner.

James Brown did not just conquer the music world. He changed it. And when he was finished everybody was imitating him. There are artists like Michael Jackson and Prince who became famous doing James Brown's spins and splits. What was the sound of some of James Brown's contemporaries? Their sound was whatever would get them into the Copacabana or to Carnegie Hall. But James Brown said, "I'm going to those places on my own terms." And he did.

So when the media began portraying me as a buffoon, it never bothered me, because that was never who I saw myself to be. I defined myself long ago. I always defined my own terms.

There were people who were commercially more successful than James Brown for a season. But he lasted. He never compromised his sound. He never watered down who he was. Today everybody in the world knows the James Brown sound. He's the Godfather of Soul. When he said, "Say It Loud, I'm Black and I'm Proud," the world said it back. And because of him, everybody knows Al Sharpton.

CHAPTER NINETEEN

★

FREDDY'S AND THE ANTI-SEMITISM QUESTION

When I was growing up, people were talking about burning down the country. When I was growing up, most of my friends in Brooklyn who went to Brooklyn College with me were wearing fatigues, wearing Chairman Mao buttons, and talking about overthrowing the government. That was the norm; that wasn't the exception. I was considered a moderate because I believed in the system. They didn't believe in the system at all. And I'm talking about white kids—who were into the antiwar movement, calling cops pigs. When they saw police drive by, they would say, "Oink, oink, oink!" But I'm extreme?

In 2002 they had the World Economic Conference in New York City. There was such a security uproar because when they had the conference in Seattle there were riots and violent demonstrations and they feared the same in New York. You have never seen a speck of violence at a march or demonstration that I led. But they call me disruptive.

The only violence I ever experienced in twenty-five years of marching and protesting was when a guy stabbed me. And even then, I kept the crowd from reacting.

Some people say, "Well, what about Freddy's." That's a good example of how my image is distorted. None of my demonstrations against Freddy's, nor anything I did concerning the demonstrations against Freddy's, led to his store being burned down and many innocent people losing their lives. That was the act of one deranged man, who not only did not have ties to me or my organization but was also one of my biggest critics.

Freddy Harari, who owned Freddy's Fashion Mart, subleased space to Sikhulu Shange's Record Shack. Freddy raised the rent, making it impossible for the Record Shack to stay in business in that space. I felt Freddy's was pushing Sikhulu out, and we would not stand for that.

Here was a guy, Sikhulu Shange, who had a record store in our community for twenty years. He was South African and a friend of the Mandelas. His store was right in front of the Apollo Theater. I grew up buying from Sikhulu Shange. When James Brown used to play the Apollo, we would go across the street afterward and buy records from the Record Shack. It was a neighborhood institution.

I came to know about Freddy's not just because of Mr. Shange, but some of the workers from Freddy's came to us complaining about unfair labor practices there. Some of the workers—blacks and Latinos—told me that Freddy was paying them off the books, way below minimum wage, and that there were hazardous conditions in the store. In fact, Freddy was cited by the City of New York for hazardous conditions.

In September 1995, I held a rally at the National Action Network, and in my radio broadcast I supported a boycott of Freddy's Fashion Mart.

I said, "We will not stand by and allow them to move this brother so that some white interloper can expand his business on 125th Street. And we're asking the Buy Black Committee to go down there, and I'm gonna go down there, and do what is necessary to let them know that we are not turnin' 125th Street back over to outsiders as it was done in the early part of this century."

Yes, I referred to Freddy as a "white interloper." And that was wrong. I should not have used the word "white," because that made the whole thing racial. But Freddy was clearly an interloper—someone who took from the community and did not give back. He was using the community.

We protested his store, and in addition to calling him out for his labor practices, we said if he evicted Sikhulu we were going to continuously boycott and picket his store.

Some extreme conservatives took our stance as my not wanting whites on 125th Street. That wasn't the case. Why would I wait all those years and just pick on Freddy? There were many white businesses and building owners on 125th

Street then and now. Why hadn't I targeted any other white businesses for boycott before Freddy's or since Freddy's? I rent space myself from a white person on 125th Street for National Action Network. Having whites on 125th Street has never been the issue.

There was a guy in the community who was always attacking me and screaming craziness like, "Y'all out here marching all the time with that nonviolent Martin Luther King stuff. We need to take arms!" This is the guy who allegedly went in and torched Freddy's in December. How can you connect a statement I made in September and say that it incited someone to violence in December? There was no demonstration that day, no march, no speeches. But at about ten o'clock that morning, this guy goes up there by himself, shoots several workers in Freddy's, and starts a fire that ends up killing him and the workers who weren't shot—who happened to be black and Hispanic. And somehow Sharpton is to blame? What that man did was an act brought on by his own mind.

In 1998 a group of construction workers held a demonstration down Madison Avenue in midtown Manhattan that got out of hand. Several police officers got attacked and they even punched a mounted police horse. There were several candidates for mayor there to show their support for the construction workers. Did they get blamed for the outbreak of violence? No one said their support incited the riot.

I wasn't even at the scene three months later when that guy burned down Freddy's. No one in the community connected me to the fire. They knew what happened. None of the family members of the victims of the fire implicated me. They sued Freddy and the city. They didn't sue me. Because they knew I had nothing to do with it. My only role was in fighting for justice in the same nonviolent manner I have my entire career.

The whole idea of my inciting violence is absurd. But someone will say, "What about Crown Heights?" Once again, a serious distortion of the truth.

Crown Heights happened when two kids were in front of their house playing in Brooklyn. A car jumps the curb and kills one of the kids. A private Jewish ambulance comes to take care of the driver of the car and leaves the two little children. The little boy dies and the driver flees the country. Violence breaks out. That night, Yankel Rosenbaum, a Jew, is killed.

I grew up near Crown Heights and was born in Crown Heights at Kings County Hospital. But at the time of this incident, I was living in Englewood, New Jersey, and had not even heard about the incident that happened there until the next day.

I was in Harlem, eating at Sylvia's, when my office called me on the cell phone and said that a Mr. Cato wanted to speak with me. Mr. Cato was the father of a little boy who was mowed down and killed by the car that jumped the curb in Crown Heights the night before. They connected me to Mr. Cato. He asked me if I would come to Crown Heights to see him and help his family seek justice.

Yankel Rosenbaum, a young Jewish man who was killed in a riot that broke out after little Gavin Cato and his cousin were run over, had already been dead fifteen hours before Mr. Cato even called me.

I went to Crown Heights and there was a second night of violence. I took Mr. Cato's brother to the morgue to identify little Gavin's body. He was seven years old. And I went to the hospital with him to see his daughter, who was badly hurt in the accident.

Violence erupted in Crown Heights, with Hasidic Jews on one side of Eastern Parkway throwing rocks and bottles, and those from the West Indian community on the other side throwing rocks and bottles.

David Dinkins and I had to cross paths again. We were still a little distant around this time, and after I was called into Crown Heights there were those around him who felt it would be touchy for him to appear to be negotiating with me. But I wasn't there to negotiate anything. I was simply representing the Cato family, who had lost their son.

So after some interplay back and forth, there was a move to bring us together. The mother of Ed Townes, a congressman from Brooklyn, died. I grew up with Townes and was going to the wake and funeral. And as a public official, Dinkins was also going to pay his respects. There was a compromise for us to meet at the wake of Townes's mother. And we talked there for the first time in years.

After the wake, we met up at Restoration Plaza and continued to talk. We reached a meeting of the minds. I agreed that I would hit the streets to restore peace if he would appeal to the police department to be fair and evenhanded in their treatment of blacks and Hasidics in Crown Heights. At the time, police were arresting only blacks for the violence that erupted there. The violence was clearly coming from both sides.

The first night I got out to Crown Heights, someone threw two rocks at us. I said, "You can't *not* arrest them! You have to have balance."

We brought in some of the mothers and some of the kids who were arrested, and they went off on Dinkins. He was really pained, really torn up about what was happening there. I think people were being totally unfair in saying that Dinkins didn't do all that he could to try and keep the violence down. He did everything anyone could do. The violence was out of control on both sides. And within a day and a half, he got the police under control. And I hit the streets and started squashing the violence on my end.

History will say that Crown Heights was one of David Dinkins's downfalls. But if you compare the violence there to the riots in Los Angeles following Rodney King, or to what went down in Miami, there is no comparison. Crown Heights was nothing compared to the violence in other cities involving similar circumstances. I think certain political figures shaded the truth because they just didn't want to see him as mayor.

For anyone to try and act like David Dinkins was anti-Semitic is crazy. Dave Dinkins is and was probably more pro-Jewish than some Jews themselves. I think some really resented this man, no matter how fair he was, no matter how decent he was, no matter what he did. They just didn't like the idea of his being mayor.

Dave Dinkins did not fail as mayor of New York. I think that he took over the city at a very tumultuous time. And he did as good a job or better than anybody could have at that time. I think it was a very difficult time—the economy was bad, there was a lot of polarization that had started under Koch's watch. And I think Dinkins really started getting ahold of the city. Then he was voted out. Under Dinkins, crime had started going down, and a lot of the initiatives he put in place laid the foundation for what Rudy Giuliani was able to take credit for. Giuliani was a demagogue in many ways, especially in how he played Crown Heights and how he played up the polarization of the city and the economy. You have to remember that the Clinton years of prosperity had just started. Clinton was elected in 1992. And in so many ways, Dinkins didn't get a chance to enjoy the flowers that resulted from the seeds he planted. Ironically, Giuliani was able to benefit from some of the overall national success in lowered crime rate and improved economy. Giuliani was lucky. And David Dinkins's mayoralty should not be defined by Crown Heights.

But that's history. History had me out in Crown Heights fanning the flames and inciting the violence that ultimately led to the death of Yankel Rosenbaum. I didn't even know there was a Yankel Rosenbaum until well after he was killed.

But it is in the interest of those who don't want to deal with the issues at hand to distort the facts. There is no doubt in my mind that if I had incited violence in Crown Heights they would gladly have indicted me, with pleasure. But they did not because I did not.

It's much easier to paint someone with a certain brush than to deal with the truth that they represent. As a result of Freddy's and Crown Heights, there are those who have called me an anti-Semite.

In fact, I am not alone—a lot of black leaders have been branded with this bogus charge. It's time to expose the hypocrisy. No, real anti-Semitism was on display between President Richard M. Nixon and Rev. Billy Graham. With the recent release of the White House tapes and transcripts of the conversation between Nixon and Graham, it's time for America to stop the hypocrisy and be outraged over that.

In 1972, Graham told Nixon in the Oval Office after a prayer breakfast that Jews had too much power and that "this stranglehold has got to be broken or the country's going down the drain." Graham also said that "they're [the Jews are] the ones putting out the pornographic stuff." On the tapes that were released in February 2002, Nixon is heard referring to Jews as "kikes." This was the president of the United States and one of the most revered religious and spiritual leaders in this nation having a discussion about how Jews were taking over and running the country and how to stop them from controlling the media. And they call me an anti-Semite?!

Graham, the picture of American religion, sat there and said, "My Jewish friends don't know how I feel about them." And there was no public outcry about his statements. No one condemned him. And he still gets municipal stadiums—on the taxpayers' dime—to hold his crusade. Nixon was just as guilty on those tapes, yet no one has stood up and said that the federal government should take Nixon's name off anything that has federal funding, including the Nixon Library.

But we had the United States Senate vote to denounce people like Louis Farrakhan, who never sat in the halls of power. Farrakhan has never been an elected official—was never elected to serve and protect all people—yet he was vilified and denounced by the Senate while Nixon was given a free pass.

Jesse Jackson referred to New York as "hymietown" more than twenty years ago and he's still trying to live that down. And Billy Graham gets a free pass?

I am constantly defending myself against the anti-Semite label for statements I didn't even make—yet we had a sitting president conspiring against Jews with the biggest preacher in the country, in the official residence of the president, and nobody opens their mouth? I dare somebody to bring anti-Semitism into the presidential race of 2004.

To this day, Billy Graham and Richard Nixon are being held up as American heroes. Where were the Joe Liebermans and the others in the United States Senate when those tapes and transcripts came out? But every black leader has to be asked about his or her relationship with Louis Farrakhan or Khalid Muhammad.

Why doesn't every Republican have to answer about Richard Nixon? Why doesn't every televangelist have to answer about Billy Graham? Why don't we play the game by the same set of rules?

Billy Graham and Richard Nixon were not making some off-color remark. This wasn't a slip-up in a speech or a stupid, hurtful remark made in a private conversation with a reporter. This was the president and a preacher—power—conspiring against Jews, in the White House.

Until America deals with this, I don't want to hear any more about black leaders being anti-Semitic. It's hypocritical and it shows just how far people are willing to go to drive a wedge between blacks and Jews. The whole labeling of black leaders as anti-Semites is not even about anti-Semitism; it's about dividing and conquering.

CHAPTER TWENTY

★

THE MOVEMENT

There are many who question what I do. And I will tell them it is necessary. Without activism, without this Movement, so many would go without justice. But activism is not without lessons and growth.

The first major protest I ever led was the march on Howard Beach in 1986. It was the first case that began to project nationally our use of direct-action strategies in the North. Dr. King used this very effectively to make changes in the South during the Civil Rights Movement, but it had never really been used effectively in the North until Howard Beach.

We marched into the white community there and exposed hostility and racism from the open "Nigger!" calls to the watermelons. It was effective and led to the arrests and convictions of John Lester, the ringleader who chased and beat Michael Griffith and four others.

This was the time when we started honing our street-legal strategy with lawyers Alton Maddox and C. Vernon Mason. My team would mobilize the streets with our marches and protests while Maddox and Mason would take care of business in the courts. It was a very effective combination. And it started in Howard Beach.

The lawyers needed the street drama to make the prosecutors and the system understand that the public will be paying attention to these cases. If these cases were tried in a closet, the way others had been, they would play all kinds of games.

The community needed good lawyers because you can have all the hell-raising you want outside, but if you don't have someone fighting for you in the courts, who knows how to deal with the law, you will never see any justice. You would have a lot of motion and no movement. There had to be balance.

We began to hone that balance in Howard Beach. And we perfected it in Bensonhurst. In 1989, Yusuf Hawkins, a sixteen-year-old, was in Bensonhurst, Brooklyn, following up on an ad he had seen for a car. He got into an altercation with a gang of white boys, who accused him of talking to one of their women. They fought, and Yusef Hawkins was shot to death.

We had marched for twenty-nine days in Bensonhurst, Brooklyn. We marched there for justice because for twenty-nine days the people of Bensonhurst kept quiet. They knew who killed Yusuf Hawkins. There were people in the community who were part of the attack, and no one would give them up. We marched there to say, "Give them up! Tell who did it." Our marches led to the arrests of four people, including ringleader Keith Mondello. We were getting action. In addition to solidifying the movement, Bensonhurst became a turning point in my career. It became the place where I had to come face to face with whether I was willing to die for the Movement—literally.

On the twenty-ninth day of our marches through Bensonhurst, on a Saturday, we went through our usual procedure. We came through the frozen zone that the police had set up for us to protect us from the violent crowd there. Protestors began unloading from the buses while police cars surrounded this area behind a local public school. We needed the protection because the folks from Bensonhurst were not only hurling insults, but they were throwing things like watermelons at the protestors. On this particular Saturday, I had arrived in a car. I got out of my car to get together with the protestors. I turned to say something to Moses Stewart, Yusuf Hawkins's father, and I felt something brush past me. Out of the corner of my eye, I caught this guy running away. I remembered his face; he had a contorted look of hatred on his face. And I thought to myself, "That guy just punched me!" I looked down at my chest where I thought he'd punched me, and saw this object sticking out of my chest. It was a knife.

I said, "Oh, my God!" and I pulled it out. And when the air hit the wound, I went down. I was all right until I realized I was stabbed. I was down and blood was everywhere and people started screaming. There were two hundred police there and a police trailer, but no ambulance. So they threw me into one of the civilian cars with a cop and they put a police patrol car in front of us to rush us through the traffic to get to the hospital. I'm in the police car with a rookie cop. He looked at me and said, "Oh, God, I hope there wasn't poison on that knife." Now, that was the last thought on my mind until he brought it up. It wasn't exactly the most comforting guy they could have sent to the hospital with me. When I got to the hospital, I was thrown onto a gurney, and that's when I came to terms with the possibility that I might not make it. I had lost a lot of blood, and the knife had penetrated just inches from my heart. I made up my mind right there that if I was to die, I was fine with it. That's when I realized I was willing to die for justice. It's one thing to say something like that. But I've been at the point of death; I've been to jail; I've had public disgrace with Tawana Brawley; and each time, I know in my heart of hearts that I don't care what they do, what they say, what they write—I believe in what I'm doing. I never ever said, "God, if you get me out of this I'll do something else," or "I'm sorry I did this." I have no regrets.

CHAPTER TWENTY-ONE

★

TAWANA BRAWLEY

I have marched for justice in Howard Beach. I have marched for justice in Bensonhurst. I have fought for justice for men like Abner Louima and Amadou Diallo. I shed a light on racial profiling throughout this country. I have spent ninety days in prison in protest over the bombings in Vieques. I have even fought for justice for the workers of Enron who were scammed out of their life savings. But the one case that seems to take more precedence over every good I have done in my career is Tawana Brawley. There are whole Web sites devoted to the topic. And for some, that case defines my career and is the sole reason why I should not be supported by anyone in this country. For me, it defines my character, because I refused to bend or bow—no matter the pressures. I took the word of a young girl, and if I had it to do over, I would do it again.

If I am elected president of the United States, I will appoint an attorney general. Is the public saying to me that if the attorney general does not win every case he or she fights, I ought to resign as president? What does that have to do with Tawana Brawley? Two lawyers told me that the evidence was strong and they believed that Tawana Brawley was telling the truth. I came into the case, as did Bill Cosby and others, believing that what Ms. Brawley said happened to her. And I still believe there was enough credible evidence for this to go to trial. It did not. We lost. Should I then stop doing my work, stop fighting against injustices in this country? We were sued for libel by Stephen Pagones, one of the men identified by Tawana Brawley as being responsible for the rape and other violations she said happened to her. Pagones accused us of making up the entire story and purposely defaming his name. What the jury found was that there was no conspiracy. They said, "We believe that Sharpton was misled." (I don't believe I was misled.) But if the jury in the libel case had said that they believed we set out and made this story up, then there would be a credible question of my character.

We were found guilty of making statements that the jury felt the evidence did not support. We paid Stephen Pagones, who said the verdict was a slap in his face because he asked for millions and got only $65,000 from me. Even the *New York Post*, Pagones's biggest supporter, said people ought to boycott Poughkeepsie, where the trial was held, because the jury said, "We hope Rev. Sharpton continues his work, but we don't feel that the evidence was here this time."

People must realize that I can get sued anytime I step out in support of any case. On the Abner Louima case, I could have been sued. Dr. King was sued several times. The whole case with *New York Times v. Sullivan* was an attempt to block Dr. King's movement. Adam Clayton Powell went out on the bag lady lawsuit. It is normal in civil rights to go through these suits. There's nothing unusual about an activist getting sued. What would be unusual is if we created a hoax. And clearly, Tawana Brawley told her story way before she met Al Sharpton. And I believed her.

I must now challenge America. People say, "Fine, you believed her and when the jury came back and didn't believe her, when they came back and said no case, why did you continue?" How many Americans believe O. J. Simpson is guilty? So they have a right to disagree with a jury, but I do not? How many white Americans today don't care what that jury said about O. J. being not guilty, and say, "O. J. Simpson is guilty!" The O. J. case was a criminal trial on television, and still people disagree with the verdict. The Tawana Brawley case never got to a trial. By what rules do I have to agree with a jury, yet they don't have to? Legally, O. J. Simpson is not a murderer.

Geraldo Rivera, one of O. J. Simpson's biggest critics, came to Poughkeepsie, New York, to testify for me, and they wouldn't let him. He came there to say, "I'm here not because I believe Brawley, but I want to know: what's the difference between what Sharpton did and what I did? To this day I call O. J. a murderer. Because that's what I believe. And Sharpton has the same right."

I didn't know Stephen Pagones from Adam. To think that I was sitting in New York, had just finished the Howard Beach case—one of the biggest victories of my career—and I would pick some obscure guy a hundred miles up the road who I had never heard of, and decide to make up this story about him, is absurd. I believed Tawana Brawley. I had never heard of Stephen Pagones. People act like Stephen Pagones was some household name. He wasn't Rudy Giuliani, and I had a beef with him. I had never heard of him. Just like I didn't know who Justin Volpe—the police officer convicted of brutalizing Abner Louima—was before I got involved with the Abner Louima case. I believe the victim.

Justin Volpe said in the beginning of the Abner Louima trial that he didn't violate Abner Louima with a stick in that police precinct bathroom. He said Abner Louima assaulted him. He kept this story almost until the end of the trial, when he finally confessed. But up until that point, was I to stop believing Abner Louima? Until the day Justin Volpe said he did it, they threw everything out there—they said Abner was a homosexual and that's how he got those injuries. I mean they said everything.

Suppose Justin Volpe had never confessed and had won the case? People would have said, "Sharpton lied on that man! There was never any sodomy." That's the risk an activist takes. I don't think people understand that this is no bed of roses. Any one of these cases can flip on you. I was sitting in my Harlem offices one afternoon in February 1999. And a guy comes in saying he's the head of a Guinean National Association. He was insisting on seeing me, saying that a young man from Guinea was shot the night before. We didn't know anything about this. It wasn't in the press yet. It was a Thursday afternoon; I'll never forget. He said, "They shot him more than forty times . . ." I said, "This is outrageous; I don't believe this." While he was trying to convince me of what happened, I got a phone call from One Police Plaza. Now, in eight years I can count on one finger the number of times anyone in the Giuliani administration called me.

They said there was a shooting in the Bronx and that I may hear about it, but everything will be all right. Then I knew something must be wrong, because the police department never called me.

The Guinean representative told me that the young man who was killed was a good kid and that he was shot for no reason. I'm still thinking, "I don't know if they are going to come out and say that this guy had drugs or a weapon." You just don't know. I took a risk and decided to believe this man.

I called for an investigation. "No matter what the circumstances (and I didn't know the circumstances), no one deserves to be shot at over forty times," I said. "You don't do that in a firing squad!"

It ended up being a legitimate case. The Amadou Diallo case is one of the most prominent instances of police over-reaction and callous disregard for life brought on by bias and bigotry in this country.

But when these cases are brought to you, you just don't know. It could have easily been the reverse, if they proved that Amadou Diallo had an Uzi in his pocket. How do you know? You don't.

I had another case one Saturday afternoon in 1998. I had just given a speech at the House of Justice, and I was heading back to my office to change my shirt because I sweat a lot when I'm speaking, and there's a guy arguing with my assistant, J. D. Livingston. He was a big, burly man and he was crying. When I got into my office, I called J. D. in and asked, "What's going on?"

"He says some state trooper shot his son in New Jersey," J. D. said. "I told him he has to have an appointment to see you."

I said, "The man is crying; just let him in and let's hear what he has to say."

The guy comes in. He shows me a little article he cut out of the *New York Times* that day where a trooper shot three kids on the New Jersey Turnpike for rolling their van back on him. And I said, "Okay, what's the problem?"

"My kid wouldn't do that," he said.

"Were you in the car?"

"No," he said. "But I know my kid wouldn't do that."

"How do you know?" I said.

"I know my kid!"

"Did they have drugs in the car?

"No."

"Guns?"

"No"

I said, "How do you know?"

"I know my kid!"

"Well, what about his friends? Maybe they had something."

He wouldn't hear it. He believed so much that they were innocent, and he wouldn't be swayed. I told him we had to look into it. He all but accosted me physically.

I said, "Okay, I tell you what, I'm on my way to Washington, D.C. (I was scheduled to preach at eight the next morning at Union Baptist Church, Rev. Willie Wilson's church.) I'm flying back to preach at twelve o'clock at Abyssinian Baptist Church in Newark, New Jersey. I'll hold a press conference, you meet me at the church and call for the complete investigation of your son's shooting.

"I cannot defend your son. But I can call for a complete investigation and justice in the matter." He said, "Fair enough." I flew into Newark, and all the press was there. And the man showed up with the driver of the van, who was the only one who wasn't shot. That ended up being the New Jersey Four case that really brought racial profiling into the national spotlight. Suppose they'd come out and found those kids had seventeen machine guns in that van? I had no way of knowing that. But I believed a man about his son, just like I believed Abner Louima. And I believed Mrs. Brawley about her daughter.

To me there is still reasonable doubt in that case. Something very bad happened to Tawana Brawley. And I will not apologize for believing her. Mr. Pagones was identified by Tawana Brawley, and I believed her. How did a fifteen-year-old girl know Stephen Pagones? Did she pull his name out of a hat? He said, "I didn't do it." She said, "He did do it." I chose to believe her.

He sued me for defamation, and in a court I was found liable for statements I made preceding the grand jury report. The statements I made were based on what I was told. Really, what they're saying is that I ought to assume that when a young lady like that comes to me, I ought to assume she is lying. I will never do that. And we are arguing that very point in our appeal of that libel verdict, which I think will be overturned. What no one will ask is, even if I believed Tawana was lying (and I don't), how would I know, before the grand jury session, that there was a question? Why would I be quiet before anyone even says, "There's no evidence here."

But on the flip side, when you see reversals like in the Abner Louima case—where three of the four officers convicted for their involvement in the cover-up of the violation and brutality of Louima were let go—you begin to question the whole justice system.

So I can't stand behind Tawana Brawley and believe her,

but the supporters of those police officers—who were convicted—have a right to stand behind their people without question?

As the son of a single mother, who had to deal with incest and violation in my own family, if I had to lose my career to stand up for a woman who said she was violated, then so be it. I'm willing to do that. If there's anything I owed, risking whatever I had, it was to stand up for a woman whom no one would listen to. That's why I never ever hesitated. I felt, "Let it go to the courts." If she's right or wrong, I will fight for her to have her say in court, because somebody has to have enough guts in this country to stand up for people who don't have a voice. I said, "Bring it to court. Prove she wasn't violated." She never got her day in court.

Folks want to use Tawana Brawley as the one thing that will bring me down. Imagine a party that would question my standing up and being sued for standing up for a young lady whom I believed was violated, but which finds room for people who have taken people's life earnings, retirement, 401K? Imagine them vilifying me and standing up for those politicians who supported Enron. Imagine them saying, "How can Al Sharpton lead the liberal wing?" when we've had all kinds of people leading in this party who had extramarital sexual relationships with young girls or had questionable relations, like Ted Kennedy, Gary Condit, and Bill Clinton. I mean, the audacity! So when people say, "Do you have hesitations running because of Brawley?" I say,

"No!" That makes me want to run even more, so they can compare what they consider my baggage to the trunks some of the leaders of the Democratic Party are carrying.

If your thing against me is that I stood up for somebody who no one else would stand up for, that pales compared to some of the personal peccadilloes that some of the Democratic *and* Republican leadership have personally been involved in. The Brawley case helped define Al Sharpton.

It was a test for me on whether or not, with all the world down on me, I would stand up for what I believe. I was told in many different ways, "Just denounce her and you will be accepted. Just denounce her and we will take you in."

At certain places in your life, I believe you are tested on whether or not you really mean what you say and say what you mean. It reminds me of a sermon I used to preach about how the devil tempted Jesus. He brought him up on the top of the mountain and told him to look out and "if you follow me, I will give you all of this." The devil said, "Just bow down, and I'll give you kingdoms of the world."

There comes a point in your life where the world will say, "Just submit and you will get anything you want." And even if you could get it, it defines who you are. Even if you get everything in the world, if you get it by bowing down, then they got you before you got it.

There is a line in James Brown's "Say it Loud; I'm Black and I'm Proud" that goes, "I would rather die on my feet than live on my knees." I believe that. I failed an oral quiz once in junior high school. The teacher asked us, "What would you rather be: A living dog or a dead lion." Everybody said a living dog, and I was the only one who said, "A dead lion." She told me I was wrong. I said, "I don't agree with that." And she asked me why. I told her, "A dog, no matter how long he lives, will never be anything but a dog. But that lion, while he was alive, he was king of the jungle. He stood for something." And I always would rather have a short life about something than a long life about nothing.

I stood up for Brawley, like I stood up for Abner Louima, Amadou Diallo, Michael Stewart, Yusuf Hawkins, the New Jersey Four, and countless others who had no one to stand up for them.

And with Brawley and everything they threw at us, I never in my own mind wavered—even knowing that it would be politically expedient to do so.

And if that girl lied, that's on her. But I wasn't going to lie about my belief in her.

CHAPTER TWENTY-TWO

★

AMADOU DIALLO AND RACIAL PROFILING

On February 4, 1999, a young man from Guinea who came to this country because it is known throughout the world as the land of opportunity, and who was working as a street vendor to send money back home, was killed by police.

Amadou Diallo was coming home when four police stopped him in the vestibule of his apartment building in the Soundview section of the Bronx. He apparently fit the description of a serial rapist who was reportedly spotted in Soundview. As Diallo reached into his jacket to get his wallet to show his identification, all four officers from the Special Street Crimes Unit opened fire—unloading forty-one shots on an unarmed man, hitting him nineteen times.

It was a slaughter. Amadou Diallo would not have faced forty-one bullets even if he were standing before a firing squad! It was one of the most stunning acts of violence perpetrated by the New York police since the sodomizing of Abner Louima, and for many of us it underscored the lack of value placed on the lives of black men in Rudy Giuliani's New York City. It put the issue of racial profiling even more at the center of our consciousness, and it was a wake-up call to all of black America. Amadou Diallo's only crime that night was being black. It could have been any one of us, any one of our children.

Even then-President Bill Clinton had to admit that the shooting of Diallo was racially charged when he said at a political dinner following the verdict of the four officers who were acquitted of the shooting, "I don't pretend for a moment to second-guess the jury. But I know most people in America of all races believe that if it had been a young white man in an all-white neighborhood, it probably wouldn't have happened." That's why we protested. That's why we marched. That's why we were arrested.

They moved the trial to Albany for "justice's sake," only to allow for one of the most unjust sentences in recent memory. The four white New York City police officers, charged with murder, were acquitted by a New York State Supreme Court jury of seven white men, one white woman, and four black women. They were acquitted of firing forty-one bullets at an innocent, unarmed man. They were acquitted of hitting him nineteen times with bullets that ripped through his lungs, his stomach, and through his heart. They were allowed to go free while the body of Amadou Diallo had to travel back to Guinea for burial.

Leading up to the trial, we organized protests and demonstrations.

The first day of protests, Rev. Wyatt T. Walker, who marched with Dr. King and who is pastor of my church, Canaan Baptist Church in Harlem, was arrested for civil disobedience along with Rev. W. Franklin Richardson and me. We decided we were going to make these protests and arrests daily events. Early on, following the shooting of Diallo there was talk about protesting at City Hall. After all, it was Giuliani's leadership (or lack of leadership) that created the environment for Diallo to be shot. But I felt that if we protested at City Hall it would look political. So we decided to protest at police headquarters at One Police Plaza because the shooting of Diallo was a policing issue.

On the first day of the protests, eight of us went to jail. The next day it was eleven, and it started growing from there. Don King was in town that weekend to promote a fight, and I attended a prefight dinner he had with the then-chairman of Time Warner, Gerald Levin. Rangel, who was also a friend of Don King, was there and came over to me and said, "You know, I think it's an outrage what happened with Diallo. I don't want to see you out there by yourself on this." He said he thought the daily protests were interesting. "I tell you what," he said. "I'm going to come go to jail with you on Monday."

I said, "You, a ranking member of Congress, dean of the New York delegation, going to jail?"

"Yeah!" he said.

"Mr. Rangel, if I put that out there I'm not going to be embarrassed, am I?"

"Put it out there," he said. "I'll be there on Monday."

The next night, David Dinkins was at the fight and he talked to one of my attorneys, Michael Hardy. "Charlie's going down to protest on Monday," he said. "Tell Al I will be there, too." When I heard this, I just knew it was a joke. There was no way that David Dinkins, first black mayor of the City of New York, was going to jail. But he did.

That Monday, both he and Rangel showed up and went to jail. From that point on, Rangel and I started having more of a relationship. Before Diallo, our relationship was cool at best. He was the man who took the seat away from my hero, Adam Clayton Powell Jr. But we forged an alliance that day that is still solid today. An injustice like the shooting of Diallo has a way of bridging gaps and healing wounds among people who ultimately have the same interests.

During our protests, more than 1000 people were arrested for civil disobedience—from the highest-ranking black elected official in New York, State Comptroller Carl McCall, to the publisher of *Essence* magazine, Edward Lewis, to NAACP national president Kweisi Mfume, to Dick Gregory, to Ossie Davis and Ruby Dee, to Oscar-winning actress Susan Sarandon, to the presidents of the largest trade unions in New York City, Dennis Rivera, of 1199 National Health and Human Service Employees Union, and Lee Saunders, Acting Chief of District Council 37 of AFSCME, to Chloe Breyer, daughter of U.S. Supreme Court Justice Stephen G. Breyer, to all of the clergy from a wide array of denominations, from Jewish rabbis to Catholic priests.

The murder of Amadou Diallo touched a nerve in many who believe in fairness and justice for all.

Unfortunately, shortly after Diallo's killing, another unarmed innocent black man was gunned down by police. It was turning into open season on black men. The case of Patrick Dorismond was particularly painful for me. Here was a guy who did what he was taught by his parents and community—to say no to dope. He comes out of a tavern after work with an associate. An undercover cop proposes a drug deal and Dorismond turns it down. They get into an argument because Dorismond is offended that the cop even proposed a drug deal to him, and the cop kills him. Why was he fighting with the cop? they said following the killing.

For one, Dorismond didn't know he was a cop—he was undercover—and two, Dorismond was rightfully offended that this guy was offering him dope. The cop should have congratulated him. Instead, he kills him and then he's not prosecuted. That was the ultimate insult. Here was a guy doing what is right, doing right so much so that he is indignant over even the hint of wrongdoing being asked of him, and he is killed by a cop. Dorismond was unarmed, so it wasn't self-defense.

When the cop saw how firm Dorismond was, he should

have stopped and said, "Wait a minute; I'm an undercover cop. You're doing the right thing." Instead, the cop gets into a fight with Dorismond and shoots him. What no one ever explained to me is why the cop was arguing with Dorismond when the cop knew it was an undercover operation. I just do not understand that. What was the point of the cop?

And then, after the killing, Giuliani adds insult to injury by revealing that Dorismond had a juvenile record, to try and act like some minor infraction Dorismond committed as a kid was justification for his being killed by a cop. His juvenile record wasn't on his forehead when the cop shot him. It was totally immaterial, and it was against the law for Dorismond's sealed juvenile record to be unsealed. But Giuliani would rather break the law to protect a cop than uphold the law to protect the people.

Again we organized protests. Now, there are some who will say all the marching and protesting were for naught because the Diallo cops went free and the Dorismond cop was never prosecuted. And while I will admit that those decisions certainly gave me a sense of discouragement, I in no way feel that our protests have been futile or for naught.

When you look at what it took, from the Montgomery boycott in 1955 until 1965, when the Voting Rights Act was finally ratified, you realize you aren't going to win a struggle the first day. But it begins a process. So what we started with the Diallo protests and before, ultimately ended with the controversial Street Crimes Unit in New York City being disbanded in April 2002. That's a fruit of our struggle.

In Cincinnati, where fifteen blacks had been gunned down by police since 1995, four days of race riots—the worst since the 1960s—touched off the very same issues we were protesting in New York. After the riots, we backed nonviolent protests there that eventually led to a series of victories, with a change in police community relations and an open discussion about racial profiling in that city.

Struggles are won over the long haul. That's why we say in the church, "The race isn't given to the swift or the strong but to those who can endure until the end." If you are looking for a quick victory, you can't get into this struggle. You have to know going in that you're going to lose some battles. You're going to lose some early battles, but you have to hang in because you must win the war. And you have no choice but to win the war. The outcomes of the Diallo and Dorismond cases were very painful. In Abner Louima, we got one police officer, who was sentenced to thirty years. But we have to stay out there until the others—whose verdicts were overturned in 2002—are brought to justice and reindicted.

If we go into this thinking one or two losses would turn us around, then we've not studied the struggle. It took a decade before Dr. King and the other civil rights activists got real change. It took almost thirty years for Mandela to see change in South Africa. We think we're going to do two marches and it's going to change everything overnight? That's absurd.

We've been marching a long time. And we've seen some

things change, and we will see a lot more changes if we keep going. The only way the oppressed ever end oppression is to be more determined than their oppressors. You've got to be more determined to be free than the oppressors are to keep you in bondage. It's a battle of wills. And you must earn your freedom by showing you're more determined. No one is going to give you anything.

I keep going because I have faith. And my faith is strengthened when I see results. To see policing as a national issue—that all over the country people are having to renegotiate how police and communities ought to deal— that's a direct result of our work. Three states—New Jersey, Missouri, and Maryland—now have racial profiling laws. Most people were saying that racial profiling didn't exist when we started our work on the issue. Now it's a household phrase.

I've been able to see some fruit borne—not nearly enough, but just enough to keep us encouraged and keep us going.

CHAPTER TWENTY-THREE

★

HIP-HOP
GENERATION

I had a discussion with a few rappers a while back, and I asked them why they use so much profanity and are so misogynistic in their music.

"Rev, we're like a mirror to society," one of the rappers said. "We are merely reflecting what we see."

"Well, I don't know about you, but I use a mirror to correct what's wrong with me," I told them. "I don't look in the mirror and see my hair messed up and my teeth need brushing and just walk out of the house that way. I use the mirror to fix me."

This hip-hop culture must use their music, their influence to correct what's wrong, not to continue to perpetuate what's wrong, not continue to promote what's wrong. They have the power to do that. And if they really want to have an impact on this society, they must change their focus and show America the best of us instead of the worst.

I went to a hip-hop conference in New York, and one of the main topics of discussion was a fight for the right to use *bitch* and *ho* in lyrics. They wanted the right to call a woman a bitch—something the slave master called black women with impunity.

With all the stuff going on in this world, all they're worried about is being able to call a woman out of her name?! That's their cause? First of all, it's wrong. But second, it is insulting. These rappers and "hip-hop impresarios" weren't worried about unemployment or the financial conditions of those who support their records and made them stars. They weren't worried about the education system that keeps too many of their fans and families in poverty. They weren't worried about voting rights. They didn't have any conferences on any of that. There wasn't one seminar entitled "Economic Empowerment" or "Jobs for the 21st Century."

No, they want the right to call somebody a *ho* or a *bitch*—somebody who brought them into this world. As far as I'm concerned, they are low-down devious nothings who aren't worth the millions of dollars young people spend to make them stars.

When I look at the hip-hop generation I am disappointed, but I also see promise. I see potential unrealized. I see tremendous power. These young people have created a culture. Their words, their spirit is so powerful that their voices have penetrated mainstream culture to the point where America's culture is intertwined with the hip-hop culture, from its language to its clothing to its music. You cannot turn on a television or watch a movie and not see the influence of hip-hop. Even suburban America has been bitten by the hip-hop bug.

Unfortunately, much of what they're selling is a fraud. They spew hedonism, misogyny, and self-hate. They glorify the prison culture, the pimp culture, and drug culture. They tell the young that they're not worthy unless they're "rocking" Chanel, Gucci, or wearing platinum and diamonds. Not only is this message immoral, but it is also flawed. It's a lie.

The most ludicrous thing in the world is to see a former rapper walking around Broadway with gold teeth and a tarnished ring, and his career is gone and he has nothing else. That's how most of these stories end, but nobody is rapping or singing about that.

These artists get huge advances from the record labels, and the first thing they do is run out and buy a big, fancy car. They buy, buy, buy what they want, and beg for what they need, and end up with nothing. I think that projecting these images to young people—the bling-bling and the showpieces—and not talking to them about real estate and land and fundamental things in life that have nothing to do with flash, is almost criminal. These so-called artists are leading our youth down a road that will ultimately lead to their destruction.

When I was working with James Brown, one of the

many things he used to preach to me was how he was in show business and how too many of his peers focused on the show and forgot about the business. These young people must be made to realize that first and foremost, they're in a business. And it's a fleeting one at that. An artist can be hot today and gone tomorrow. In the old days, you would find an artist who could be around for ten or twenty years. They had staying power. But today it's one or two years and it's over. So what happens then? What happens when they've spent all their money and their career is over? They have to plan for the days when they won't be hot. Rather than buying the most expensive cars and the biggest diamonds and the baddest watch, which in a year or two will have little or no value, why not plan for the future?

That's the message I would like to hear coming from the hip-hop community. I would like them to make records about the importance of an education and talk about social responsibility and even political power.

The hip-hop generation has the power to really change this nation for the better. It has already had a tremendous impact. There is no question that American culture has been irrevocably influenced by the hip-hop community. But the hip-hop community has stopped way short of reaching its potential. Hip-hop has already permeated the social fabric of this nation, now it can also change the politics; it can also change social policy. People in power would have to listen because their children are also walking around at home with the baggy pants, the baseball caps, and the sneakers with no laces.

If those in the hip-hop community who have so much influence would use their power, maybe we would see some real changes in this country. The question is, are those who are in leadership of the hip-hop world mature and strategic enough to take the next step?

During the rock-and-roll movement in the 1960s, you saw the switch from sex, drugs, and rock and roll to politics and social change. What started as a hippy rock movement with the likes of Janis Joplin, Jimi Hendrix, and Allen Ginsberg turned into a revolution that ended up stopping the war in Vietnam. The same people who gave us Woodstock also started a social rebellion and a cultural revolution. They literally reshaped America. They used their music, their art, and their poetry to change this country and put pressure on the power structure. Hip-hop can do the same thing. Hip-hop has already done what rock did culturally, but will it be able to have the same impact on foreign policy or other political issues? Does it even care?

Russell Simmons, who is one of the fathers of hip-hop, is attempting to put a political spin on the hip-hop movement. But we need some of the popular artists to get involved, too. I've known Russell for almost twenty-five years. He did a movie in the early 1980s called *Krush Groove*, and there were riots that broke out in several theaters in Queens where the movie was playing. They wanted to take the movie out of theaters, and I went out and protested to make sure the movie chain did not.

In the last few years, Russell has become more political. In some cases I have agreed and in other cases I have disagreed with his politics. But the question for Russell and others of the hip-hop generation is not who they're going to endorse for political office, but *what* they're going to endorse.

They cannot get caught up in personalities; it has to be bigger than that. The question is not narrow partisan politics; the question is a broad social political agenda. I hope that's what Russell and others are striving to get. Their candidate and their support must come out of a broad-based vision. It can't be "I like Joe and that's who I'm going to vote for." But it should be, "I support Ann because she follows my vision for America."

The hip-hop generation will not have a real legacy until it is able to move from the flash and the bling-bling into establishing a vision for the future of America and following through.

Despite my differences with them, I will continue to support the hip-hop community because I have faith that they will eventually reach their potential.

The first big hip-hop summit that gave birth to all the others happened right at the House of Justice and was hosted by the National Action Network. Everybody from Sean (P. Diddy) Combs to Master P to *The Source* magazine (I was probably the first non-hip-hop artist to be featured on the cover of *The Source*) came together to talk about the state of hip-hop.

I couldn't make the second hip-hop summit because I was in jail, but so many of the artists tried to come through to visit me while they were in New York. So I have an ongoing dialogue with the hip-hop community, and I believe they respect me. At our 2002 National Action Network Convention, we had a hip-hop seminar.

There's the temptation of saying, "I don't want to deal with them because they are irresponsible!" Well, I can't say that, because we're talking about our children; we're talking about our future and I'm not willing to just write them off. We must deal with them. We cannot patronize them, we must have an honest dialogue and challenge them at the same time. But then you must also be prepared to be challenged, because a lot of their negative energies are born out of the failure of the adults in our society. Their words are a warning to us. We must come together and challenge one another. We have not developed an institution to teach them a lot of the things they should know.

They don't know the struggle because we don't talk to them about it. We haven't taken them under our wings and groomed them. We've ignored them or worse, considered them not worthy of our time. And we're paying for it now. So how do they inherit a legacy they don't even know about or understand? And how do they become effective leaders when they don't see any who speak to them?

With my National Action Network, I've recently begun

to groom leaders and create a system of leadership. I push young people with promise to take charge in their neighborhoods and communities and be activists. I push, so much so that many have argued with me that I push them too hard. But I have to because I understand that unless we build a collective, we're not going to get it done. There are no messiahs.

I have changed. I grew up in the charismatic leadership movement, where one man took charge and carried a movement. That's how I started out. But that was ineffective long term because every time the leader was killed or became discredited, the movement died.

We need to focus on a new style of leadership today, and the hip-hop community will be instrumental in implementing the system. I had to change because I knew that the charismatic leadership system will not work for us anymore.

I will push the hip-hop community and challenge them to reach higher. I challenge them to stop this whole glorifying of a reckless lifestyle. And I understand the difficulties they face. I have had artists tell me that record labels won't sign them unless they have a certain image or rap about certain things. They are told, "If you don't do this, shake your booty show your tits, talk bad English and purport sex and violence, you won't get a deal."

I understand that. But there has to be some integrity, some sense of righteousness among these artists. They cannot conspire to denigrate our race for the dollar. There are some who would argue that the negative images are the ones that sell. I challenge the hip-hop community to challenge the record industry and say, "That's a lie." They told James Brown that "I'm Black and I'm Proud" would not sell. It did sell. Even white folks bought his record, and it is still being sampled today. That was thirty-four years ago. Are you telling me that America is less mature than it was thirty-four years ago?

And are you telling me that all these thugged-out, tough-guy rappers are afraid to try something new?

CHAPTER TWENTY-FOUR

★

IS BLACK AMERICA
WORTHY?

There was a groundbreaking conference held in Philadelphia in February 2002. The theme was "Where Do
We Go From Here?: Black America's Vision for Healing, Har-
mony and Higher Ground," and it was hosted by radio host
and commentator Tavis Smiley.

Black leaders, educators, politicians, and preachers were
asked to sit on various panels and discuss the future not just
of black America, but of America. On my panel, Dr. Gard-
ner Taylor, Pastor Emeritus of Concord Baptist Church, one
of the most esteemed preachers in this country and known
as the dean of black preachers, asked a very important question: "Are we worthy of the legacy we inherited?"

Look at the late nineteenth century and the early twentieth century and you see people like Booker T. Washington

and Mary McLeod Bethune—people who fought for and were able to build educational institutions when blacks were not even allowed to go to public schools in the South. Today we have all this access, and parents don't have time to make sure that their children are educated. They don't have time to find out what kind of activities they could be involved with. When you look at our commitment to education today, you must ask, "Are we worthy of the legacy we inherited?"

Look at activists like W. E. B. Dubois, the first black to earn a doctorate from Harvard, who helped found the NAACP, and Marcus Garvey, who helped define the notion that black is beautiful, and when you see Martin Luther King, Malcolm X, Medgar Evers, and the thousands who gave up their lives so we could have the simplest rights, and you look at our leaders today, the question rings: "Are we worthy of the legacy we inherited?"

When you look at music legends like James Brown and Marvin Gaye, Nina Simone, Gil Scott Heron, and Curtis Mayfield, people who used their art to help change society, to say something important about society, and then you look at our musicians today, you have to ask, "Are we worthy of the legacy we inherited?"

When you look at writers like Langston Hughes, James Baldwin, Zora Neale Hurston, Richard Wright, Gwendolyn Brooks, Sonia Sanchez, Nikki Giovanni, Ralph Ellison, Amiri Baraka, Toni Morrison, and Maya Angelou, and you look at other writers and the works they produce today, you have to question, "Are we worthy of the legacy we inherited?"

When you look at politicians like Adam Clayton Powell Jr., Shirley Chisholm, and Barbara Jordan, people who made history and used their political position to change the condition of black people, and you look at our politicians today, you have to ask, "Are we worthy of the legacy we inherited?"

When you look at our athletes like Muhammad Ali, Jesse Owens, Jackie Robinson, and Tommie Smith and John Carlos—who stood on the medal podium of the 1968 Olympics with their heads bowed and one black-gloved fist raised to show their solidarity with the Civil Rights Movement—and you see our athletes today, you have to ask, "Are we worthy of the legacy we inherited?"

When you look at Thurgood Marshall, the first African American to sit on the Supreme Court, who earned his place there through his legal victories, overcoming racism and discrimination in this country, and you look at the next African American to hold that very position, you must ask, "Are we worthy of the legacy we inherited?"

Are we worthy?

We will not be worthy until we pick up our mats and walk, as Jesus told the crippled man in Luke 5. The first thing black America must do is stop making excuses for why we aren't where we need to be and find a way to get where we must go. Those people who built our legacy didn't make excuses. They made a way out of no way. They didn't just sit around complaining about the white man; they fought the system that oppressed us. They didn't cry about racism; they marched, they died, they wrote, and they sang about overcoming it.

When I preach and speak around the country to a mostly black audience, I rarely talk about racism and profiling and things like that. Those are a given. What I say to them is, "If I come from behind this podium and knock you onto the floor, that's on me. If I come back a week later and you're still on the floor, that's on you."

Yes, racism in America may have knocked us down, but we are responsible for making sure we get back up. Racism is an overused excuse. White people and racism are not the reason why far too many blacks stay home on election day. I understand being disillusioned by the system and feeling like your vote doesn't matter, but because we don't exercise our right to vote, we leave ourselves totally out of the process.

There is no excuse for people not to exercise their right to vote—especially blacks. For blacks not to vote, it is a slap in the face to Martin Luther King. It is spitting on the graves of those four little girls who lost their lives in that church bombing in Alabama. It undermines even the principles behind why Nelson Mandela spent twenty-seven years in jail in South Africa.

People lost their lives and freedom so that we today can have rights. We were able to get the right to vote in America while black South Africans had to wait many more decades to get it. Mandela spent almost thirty years in prison because it was that important. And we have the audacity to take our right to vote for granted.

The quest in the twentieth century was for blacks to get the right to vote and thus the right to vote for blacks. The quest in the twenty-first century must be to maintain and protect that right to vote and to finally vote for the *right* blacks.

We've gone from getting blacks in office to, now, fighting to get the right blacks in office. Simply voting blacks into office is not necessarily the right thing. We've elected some who have sat there for decades and only maintained power and haven't done a thing to improve the conditions of those who elected them. In many ways they have done less than whites in similar positions. It is no great accomplishment to have a black in a powerful position just to say we have a black in a powerful position. That person must be committed to changing conditions, to making a difference, to continuing the process that King and others started in order to empower poor people. They must be worthy of the legacy they inherited.

Black folks must begin to pick ourselves up by our bootstraps and take responsibility for ourselves. Yes, there is racism. But racism doesn't make parents not apply pressure to our children to do better in school. Yes, the public school system in this country is not doing the job educating our

children, and yes, that affects blacks and Latinos disproportionately; but racism within the system cannot explain why
black parents do not show up for PTA meetings or come to
the school to check on their children during parent-teacher
conferences.

Racism doesn't explain why parents don't vote in the
school board elections or why they don't check their children's homework every night. If you want to have a fight in
my household, try and get in the way of our daughters'
homework time. Kathy will tell you, "I don't care if the
Queen of England is coming over; they must finish their
homework." No excuses.

I travel a lot, but when it's time for parent-teacher conferences, I make it my business to be there as often as possible, because it's important. And my daughters must know
that their education is important to us for it to be important
to them. Black parents must do more to instill that in our
children. So even if the system is wrong, even if the system
is racist, even if the system isn't getting the job done, that's
no excuse for us not to get the job done, too.

I was speaking at a school in the Northeast recently, and
before my speech they had a little banquet. As I'm sitting
there eating, a young lady approaches me and asks if she
could speak with me before I go on stage. She told me she
was the first person in her family ever to go to college and
she was really excited. She had been doing really well, making all A's her first semester. When she returned home for
winter break and was asked how she was doing and told

them she was making all A's, her family asked her, "Are you trying to be white?!" They ridiculed her performance as if doing well in school were something reserved for only whites.

When did failure and decadence become black culture, and success and excellence be equated only with white culture? That mentality must stop. There are children all over the country, black children, who fear being ostracized by their friends and even family for doing well in the classroom. That's crazy. Racism doesn't make you downgrade a child for doing well. Racism doesn't stop parents from checking their children's homework or attending PTA and parent-teacher meetings. Racism doesn't do that.

We have internalized the decadence that was imposed on us. We have taken that inferior moniker that was placed on us throughout slavery and Jim Crow, and we keep it around our neck as if it actually belongs to us. It's like a security blanket. A convenient excuse just in case things don't work out.

Racism doesn't make men father children, then walk away from the responsibility of raising them. According to recent reports, 70 percent of all black babies born in our country today are born out of wedlock. Racism may have provided despair, poverty, lack of education, and the conditions for that statistic, but racism certainly did not make these fathers turn their backs on their own children. No, it takes something more to walk away from a child.

I think that we have to take responsibility for ourselves.

We have to preach to our young men that they must be responsible for those they bring into this world. There is no social malady that justifies making a baby that you are not going to support and take care of. And as a child whose father walked out, I know the pain and the damage left on those children.

We can talk all we want about how hard times are and how we just have to understand. No, we don't. Times have been way harder than this, and the men of my mother's generation and her mother's generation—who had to suffer far worse indignities and discrimination and racism than we experience today—by and large stood by their families. We can't buy the excuses. We can't let one man off the hook, because there is no excuse—barring death—for leaving a child fatherless.

We have to be just as aggressive, just as hard on ourselves as we are on others. In fact, the only way we can have the moral authority to challenge others is if we first challenge ourselves. We have to be just as vocal about those who use racism as an excuse for failure as we are about the individuals and system that use racism to knock us down. We must take responsibility for ourselves. In a lot of ways we have become our own worst enemy. We don't even support one another in business, but we want to complain about how we don't get the same opportunities and we don't get the same consideration in business.

According to the latest numbers, blacks spend more

money per capita than whole nations. We spent $533 billion in 1999, up 73 percent from a decade before. Using government statistics and economic models, a study said that the total black buying power was highest in New York, at $60.9 billion, and most concentrated in the District of Columbia, with 39.1 percent of the share of all buying power. But where does that money go? It doesn't go back into the black community. Is that racism's fault? In some cases, perhaps. But often it's because black folks don't have the right mentality when it comes to spending and entrepreneurship. We are consumers rather than owners.

We must begin to ingrain in our communities the importance of entrepreneurship. Our churches and social institutions must ingrain in our children the language and the habits of ownership, of developing wealth. We must stop this renting mentality and this notion of instant gratification. We must stop looking for a handout.

I have never in my life gotten a paycheck from a white man. So in many ways, this notion of someone owing me something is foreign to me. The first paycheck I ever received was one I signed over to myself as head of my National Youth Movement. That's empowering. It is that mentality that has made me my own man. It has made it easier for me never to compromise my beliefs. I have never felt beholden to anyone.

Growing up, I watched many movements thwarted by a job. I've seen civil rights activists bought off with government jobs for as little as $30,000 a year. They would say, "Here's a job," and that would shut down the movement. I could never understand that. I was fortunate to learn about entrepreneurship and real black power at an early age. Working with James Brown taught me something that black America must also learn—to stop seeking the approval of white people or people in general and build your own image. I learned early on that if I was going to be successful, I had to define for myself my own set of standards, and I had to create my own image. I had to be me, regardless of what anyone else felt or thought about me. That's true power.

So when I came off the road with James Brown in the early 1980s around the time of Bernard Goetz—the vigilante who shot two blacks on the subway who were allegedly trying to rob him—and Ed Koch offered me a job to keep quiet, there was no hesitation on my part. You can't offer me a job. I've been traveling around the world on a private jet, carrying $300,000 and $400,000 in cash. I ain't impressed by a job.

I'm marching against injustice and they say, "We can work out a job for you," and I'm looking at them like they're crazy. "A job?! Thirty thousand dollars?! I used to carry thirty thousand dollars in one day. Who do you think you're talking to? I don't want a job; I want justice!"

Being empowered like that gave me the courage to look at each man as an equal. I don't go to any government official with my hand out, looking for a gift. I go as a man seeking what's right. And I don't have to bow my head or cower, because that's not who I am. And I don't care whether or not I'm liked. I'm not going there for that, either.

So Giuliani doesn't like me? Good—I don't like him, either. He doesn't want to talk to me? Good—I don't want to talk to him, either. I was raised to be secure enough in myself not to have to kowtow to anyone. When I deal with the white power structure, it's on my terms. When I deal with City Hall or the White House, I do so on my terms. Most times when you see a picture of me and some big politician, it is at my House of Justice. They come to Harlem. I don't go to them. You rarely see me go to any of their fund-raisers or go to their offices. You rarely see me behind them on election night. I don't go, because I don't need that kind of acceptance.

The goal of the average black—particularly a prominent black—is to be accepted by the white power structure and by white people. And I don't give a damn if they ever accept me. I have set my own standards for what's important to me.

A white supremacist is not comfortable with someone who says, "I don't really care if you ever accept me or not; I don't care if you ever embrace me or not. I am what I am and that's enough for me." A supremacist must always feel that you submit to him, which is why, while I respect and admire Rev. Jackson, I psychologically could not deal with his conceding or deferring to the White House. Somewhere along the line, we need to define ourselves for ourselves.

Racism may have knocked us down, but it is our responsibility to get back up. What I am outraged by most is the number of blacks and Latinos who have become comfortable on that floor—and who have even glorified being down. They now act as if it is our culture to be down.

Black culture isn't about doing poorly and hanging on the corners. Black culture is about—and has always been about—being able to excel beyond the odds. Black culture is people like Paul Robeson, multilingual in a time when blacks couldn't attend certain colleges. Here was a man who excelled in athletics, music, and theater but, more importantly, received his degree from Rutgers, was valedictorian of his class, and was a Phi Beta Kappa. Here was a man who was the son of a slave, who went to get a law degree from Columbia University. That's black culture.

Black culture is Mary McLeod Bethune, who went from the cotton fields of South Carolina to building her own school during a time when blacks were locked out of so many institutions.

Black culture is Marian Anderson, hitting octaves that were unparalleled, when they wouldn't allow her to sing at Constitution Hall. She didn't give up. She got to sing at the Lincoln Memorial in 1939, and she went on to become the first black person to sing at the White House and at New York's Metropolitan Opera. That's black culture.

But this new era, fueled by Hollywood and television, has reinterpreted black culture as some profane, misogynistic, gold-toothed, superspook who has done more to lower the ambitions and world views of blacks than the Ku Klux Klan.

It's bad enough when an opponent knocks you out. It's more insidious when that opponent can get you to knock yourself out. And that is what's happening today with blacks in America. We have become our own downfall because we've let others define for us who we are.

When I was growing up, the culture was a real mirror—it reflected the thinking or motivation and spirit of the community.

James Brown was singing, "Say it loud; I'm black and I'm proud." Aretha Franklin, Queen of Soul, was singing about R-E-S-P-E-C-T. We've gone from James Brown, black and proud, to a group called Niggas with Attitude. We've gone from the Queen of Soul talking about respect to calling our women bitches and ho's in records! We've gone from Muhammad Ali facing jail for standing up against a war to Mike Tyson going to jail for rape. Something's wrong with that shift. It would be therapy for black America if it would not focus on the racism of society—for that will be there. We must focus on ourselves, looking in our mirrors and fixing ourselves first.

Racism may make the workplace and housing market unequal. But racism doesn't make you put gold teeth in your mouth, spending thousands of dollars when you don't have enough food to feed your family. Racism doesn't make you buy a new, expensive car when you don't own the home you live in. Racism doesn't make you make babies that you aren't going to raise and support both financially and spiritually. Racism doesn't do that.

We must take responsibility for ourselves. We may not have put ourselves on the floor, but we damn sure better learn how to get up. And until we do, the question remains, "Are we worthy of the legacy we inherited?"

INDEX